BORDERLINE PERSONALITY DISORDER GUIDE:

"Discover PRACTICAL BPD THERAPY STRATEGIES to Master Your Emotions, Build Healthy Relationships , and Enhance Your Well-Being Through DBT/CBT Skills Daily."

Dr. Riley Thompson Brooks

<u>DISCLAIMER:</u>

The information contained in this book is for informational and educational purposes only. It is not intended to be a substitute for professional medical advice, diagnosis, or treatment. Always seek the advice of your physician or other qualified healthcare provider with any questions you may have regarding a medical condition.

TABLE OF CONTENTS

PREFACE

Have you ever had the impression that your emotions are strong forces that may sometimes be too much to handle and make it hard to connect with other people? Have you experienced conflicting self-images, intense relationships, and overpowering emotions? Then you are not alone. Although borderline personality disorder (BPD) might present many difficulties, it need not define you.

This book is your all-in-one resource for understanding BPD and discovering your amazing inner powers. Here, we'll set out on a self-discovery trip to provide you with useful tools to deal with BPD's obstacles and create a more satisfying existence.

You will find evidence-based strategies based on Dialectical Behavior Therapy (DBT) and Cognitive Behavioral Therapy (CBT) on these pages. These treatments provide effective resources for:

Master Your Emotions: Acquire the necessary abilities to control strong emotions and create constructive coping strategies. You'll learn how to control your impulsive actions, manage your emotions, and develop composure in the face of adversity.

Create Strong, Supportive Relationships: Learn how to communicate effectively with those you love in order to build strong, supportive relationships. Effective communication is essential, and this book will provide you with the skills you need to express yourself honestly and freely while also encouraging empathy and understanding in the people around you.

Boost Your Well-Being: Learn about all encompassing techniques to foster self-compassion, strengthen your resilience, and create a life that has meaning and purpose. Self-care is crucial, and this book will provide suggestions on developing wholesome routines, fostering self-worth, and leading a morally upright life.

This book is about empowerment; it goes beyond theory. You'll discover ideas to put the strategies you learn into practice, real-world examples that speak to your experiences, and continuous support to help you deal with the day-to-day difficulties brought on by BPD.

This thorough guide gives you the information and resources you need to properly manage your symptoms, regardless matter whether you've just received a diagnosis or are looking for a deeper understanding of your BPD. You can create the kind of life you deserve—one that is full of deep relationships, emotional stability, and a solid sense of self—if you put in the regular work and take advantage of the encouraging advice provided here.

Together, let's start your road of change. This book is your travel buddy, an invaluable resource that will support you at every turn. You have the capacity for amazing progress, and you are not alone. Together, let's unleash it.

INTRODUCTION

Have you ever had feelings that seem all over the place? Feeling good one moment and depressed the next? You or someone you know may have been diagnosed with borderline personality disorder (BPD). BPD can be very difficult to manage since it causes strong emotions, strained relationships, and impulsive behavior. It can cause confusion and frustration in you and others around you, making you feel as if you're caught in a perplexing loop.

Those treatment sessions you can remember from the past? Yes, they can be pretty beneficial, but sometimes they come off as stodgy and fail to convey the BPD experience. This book is not like the others. Instead of flowery language, we will be concentrating on practical techniques and advice that you can use in your daily life.

I am a therapist, and I have spent many hours helping my patients navigate the complexity of Borderline Personality disease (BPD). I am aware of the significant effects BPD has on those who have been diagnosed with the disease as well as those who are close to them. Feelings of bewilderment, irritation, and even hopelessness might arise from the strength of the emotions, the mood swings that appear out of control, and the difficulties in relationships. Conventional methods cannot always be able to fully convey the complex dynamics involved with BPD.

When it comes to comprehending and managing Borderline Personality Disorder (BPD), this book have you covered. To assist both individuals with BPD and those who support them, it all comes down to combining certain tried-and-true therapeutic techniques with practical advice. This book explores the mechanisms behind borderline personality disorder (BPD), including potential causes and factors that can complicate life for those who live with it. Being aware of these things might make you feel less like you're alone and more at ease with yourself.

Managing such enormous sentiments is one of the major topics this book addresses. It incorporates some useful tips from treatments like Dialectical Behavior Therapy (DBT) to enable you to smoothly navigate such emotional turbulence.

However, it's also about how you relate to other people; it's not just about you. We're giving you advice on how to communicate so that other people will understand your perspective, which can significantly reduce conflict in your relationships. Not to mention the importance of taking care of oneself. We're going to talk about self-care practices that will keep you well and prevent burnout. To keep everyone in a positive place, we're also talking about creating boundaries within your support group. This book demonstrates that although BPD might be somewhat mysterious, it also emphasizes optimism. With the information and abilities you'll acquire, you'll be able to make everyone affected by BPD feel happier.

A preview of the topics covered in this book is provided below:

·   ***Crack the Code on BPD:*** We'll go over the main characteristics of BPD, possible causes, and related difficulties that you or a loved one could experience.

·   ***Create an Emotional Toolbox:*** Discover useful techniques from Dialectical Behavior Therapy (DBT) and other research-proven therapies to better handle strong emotions, develop self-compassion, and confidently resolve conflicts with others.

·   ***Unlock the Power of Communication:*** We'll go over techniques for communicating directly and aggressively, encouraging understanding, and minimizing conflict in your relationships.

·   ***Accept the Value of Self-Care:*** As you go through this journey, learn how to safeguard your well-being, strengthen your resilience, and refuel your emotions.

·   ***Build a Supportive Network:*** We'll look at how to build a cooperative support system that upholds appropriate boundaries for all parties.

Recall that you are not defined by BPD. It's only a segment of your tale. The goal of this book is to empower you to take charge, create coping strategies, and create a life you enjoy. It's a trip, to be sure, but we'll be doing it together one step (or even a huge leap!) at a time.

CHAPTER 1

Into the Depths: Getting to Know BPD

What is Borderline Personality Disorder?

Among the 10 personality disorders included in the DSM-IV-TR, Borderline Personality Disorder (BPD) stands out in our investigation of the intricacies surrounding mental health. These conditions are defined by persistent, deeply rooted characteristics that profoundly affect a person's capacity to function in day-to-day life. These characteristics, which are often noticeable by early adulthood or even youth, harden and result in maladaptive patterns of behavior, perception, and interpersonal interactions.

A crucial difference exists between personality disorders and other mental health illnesses such as schizophrenia or depression. In the DSM-IV-TR, personality disorders are categorized under Axis II, while the majority of other mental diseases fall under Axis I. This discrepancy is a reflection of a basic difference in our understanding of these circumstances. Axis I diseases are traditionally thought to be medication-responsive, time-limited, and perhaps related to biological variables. Between bouts, people can usually resume their "normal" functioning as the symptoms lessen.

Contrarily, personality disorders—BPD in particular—usually show themselves as persistent tendencies that don't go away even when the current issue is resolved. A longer duration of therapy is frequently necessary for effective results since it involves changing deeply ingrained behavioral habits. Studies indicate that compared to some Axis I illnesses, such as severe depression, personality disorders—particularly borderline personality disorder (BPD)—can have a more significant effect on day-to-day functioning. This emphasizes the special difficulties these diseases provide for people with mental illnesses as well as mental health providers.

As a psychotherapist, I have helped many people navigate the complex maze of mental health. One disorder that is especially fascinating and often misunderstood is borderline personality disorder (BPD). Enthralling because it represented an intriguing interaction between strong emotions, intricate relationships, and an ongoing quest for self-definition Misunderstood due to the stigma and misinformation around it. This chapter is our first road map, a compass to help us navigate the complex landscape of BPD and provide us with the means of discovery.

DISPELLING THE MYTHS OF BPD

It is important to debunk some of the myths and misunderstandings surrounding borderline personality disorder (BPD) before exploring its complexities. BPD is neither a moral failing nor a sign of weakness. Persistent patterns of instability in emotions, interpersonal connections, self-image, and behavior are the hallmarks of this complex mental health illness. Consider a range of emotional dexterity. People on one end are quick to modify their behavior to deal with various circumstances. On the other hand, people with BPD often find themselves at the other extreme, struggling with rigid patterns in their thoughts, actions, and interactions with the outside world.

Three important domains are where these patterns mainly appear:

Interpersonal Relationships:

A person with borderline personality disorder (BPD) can find relationships to be like a delicate ballet, with intense idealization and devasting devaluation occurring constantly. They might experience deep intimacy with someone else over a short period and believe that person to be unique and flawless. This extreme idealization might result in clinging and possessive actions as a frantic effort to cling to this imagined perfection. But even the smallest perceived betrayal or disappointment can set off a chain reaction that devalues that same person completely and causes extreme wrath. Often called "splitting," this emotionally intense dance can make it difficult to maintain stable and satisfying partnerships. It's possible for partners to feel like they're always treading carefully and wondering when things will get better.

Self-Image:

A person with BPD can have a constantly shifting internal environment. The very substance of who you are, your basic sense of self, might seem elusive and constantly shifting. Feelings of emptiness, uncertainty about one's values and objectives, and a persistent need for outside validation to define oneself might result from this. Attempting to construct a home on a sand foundation would be unstable and uncomfortable. This identity crisis might show itself as persistent changes in look, profession, or even worldview.

Regulating Emotions:

BPD patients' emotions can be erratic and unexpected, like a roiling sea. Emotions that are strong and fast to erupt, such as anger, despair, or excitement, can overwhelm the person experiencing them as well as others around them. Having trouble controlling these emotional swings can have a big influence on day-to-day living. Imagine trying to make a sensible choice in the middle of a furious emotional tempest; it's almost impossible. Impulsive actions, self-harm, or poor interpersonal connections can result from this.

The shadow of borderline personality disorder (BPD) is rather lengthy. As a psychotherapist, I have personally seen the toll that this misdiagnosed illness has on people who are trying to become well. Isolation, humiliation, and despair can be brought on by stigma and misconceptions. In addition to debunking some of the most widespread misconceptions about BPD, I want to provide a message of hope and support.

We start with our study by busting the most widespread misconceptions about BPD:

Myth 1: Having a BPD indicates weakness

This false belief portrays BPD as a personality defect or a lack of willpower. The reality is far more nuanced. The complex interaction of heredity and environment leads to BPD. Individuals diagnosed with Borderline Personality Disorder (BPD) can be susceptible to emotional dysregulation, a strong fear of abandonment, and a brittle sense of self due to early life traumas such as abuse, neglect, or invalidation. It takes tremendous fortitude to traverse a world of intense emotions and ongoing self-doubt when one has BPD. Imagine fighting a persistent sensation of emptiness while going through periods of extreme ecstasy and severe misery. This is the situation that many people with BPD face. Strength is the fortitude to keep going on in the face of difficulties, not the lack of battle.

Myth #2: Those who suffer from BPD are manipulative

The severe abandonment dread that characterizes BPD can sometimes result in manipulative actions. For instance, if a loved one attempts to leave, a person with BPD can threaten to commit suicide or self-harm. Beneath this frantic behavior, however, is an intense yearning for connection and a deep-seated dread of being alone. It's important to comprehend the underlying feelings. We might see the action as a cry for help and a twisted effort to provide emotional safety rather than as manipulative behavior. We should foster healthy communication and establish trust when we approach the problem with empathy and a readiness to listen.

Myth#3: It's impossible to cure BPD

This myth has the potential to be quite dehumanizing. It is quite possible to treat BPD using evidence-based treatments like as dialectical behavior therapy (DBT). People with BPD can gain important skills for controlling their emotions, reining in their actions, and forming wholesome relationships via DBT. DBT gives people the skills they need to be conscious, emotionally stable, tolerant of discomfort, and successful in social situations. It's an empowering and self-discovery quest. Even though BPD is a lifetime diagnosis, people can significantly improve their quality of life, create better coping skills, and forge deeper connections with it if they are committed to it and have the help they need.

Myth #4: Having BPD Precludes You from Living a Fulfilling Life

It's just not true what people think. Many people with BPD have successful, happy lives. Think of those who find strength and meaning in assisting others, or artists who direct their energy into creative expression. BPD does not limit your possibilities. Although it is an element of your tale, it need not write the conclusion. You can create healthy coping strategies, forge lasting connections, and accomplish your objectives with the correct support network, self-compassion, and therapy. Imagine living in a world where you can successfully control your emotions, overcome obstacles with fortitude, and be in loving, healthy relationships. With BPD, this is achievable.

Myth#5: Only Women Are Affected by BPD

For a long while, women were diagnosed with Borderline Personality Disorder (BPD) significantly more commonly than males. One myth that has been perpetuated by this historical pattern is that BPD is gender-specific. But the truth is much more complicated. Here's why this misconception endures and why it's critical to identify BPD in people of all genders:

<u>Men's Underdiagnosis of BPD:</u>

· **Variations in Presentation:** Symptoms of BPD can present differently in males than in women. Whereas males can bury their problems or express them via dangerous actions (violence, drug misuse), women can display their emotional discomfort more publicly (by sobbing or loudly expressing displeasure). Men can be more difficult to diagnose with BPD due to these external features.

·   ***Social Discrimination:*** Open emotional expression by guys might be challenging for them due to societal norms around masculinity. The stigma attached to males displaying vulnerability might serve as an additional deterrent to seeking care for mental health issues. Men with BPD can suffer in silence as a result, going undetected.

Myth #6: Bipolar disorder or schizophrenia is a form of BPD

Although BPD and other mental health disorders have some similarities, it is a separate diagnosis. For example, hallucinations and escapes from reality are characteristics of schizophrenia that are not usually present in BPD. Mania and depressive episodes are a part of bipolar illness, although BPD mood fluctuations are often quicker and more transient. For an accurate diagnosis and successful treatment, it is essential to comprehend the unique criteria associated with each ailment.

Beyond the Diagnostic and Statistical Manual of Mental Disorders (DSM)

Other personality dysfunctions, such as dependent, schizotypal, antisocial, histrionic, and narcissistic personality disorders, and BPD, have many traits in common. But what separates BPD from these other character disorders is the combination of self-destructiveness, persistent feelings of emptiness, and intense fears of abandonment. BPD is characterized by impulsivity and instability in relationships, emotions, and self-image. These are widespread patterns of behavior that often start in adolescence and last for long periods. The DSM-IV-TR (which is widely used globally) bases the diagnosis on the nine criteria listed below. To be diagnosed with BPD, a person has to have five of these nine symptoms. There are nine criteria for diagnosing BPD in the Diagnostic and Statistical Manual of Mental Disorders, Fifth Edition (DSM-5). Although these criteria provide a structure for comprehending the disorder, it's crucial to keep in mind that BPD is a lived experience rather than a strict inventory. The particular methods in which these requirements materialize might vary greatly among individuals. Here's a deeper look at some of the difficulties people with BPD can face:

Criteria 1: Intense Attempts to Prevent Actual or Perceived Abandonment

Think of balancing on a tightrope over a huge chasm. This precariousness perfectly encapsulates the universal dread of abandonment that is the basis of this criterion. Even a little perceived fear of separation—real or imagined—can cause extreme anxiety and despair in a person with borderline personality disorder (BPD). This dread can appear in many ways:

• ***Clinging and Possessive tendencies: An*** intense desire for security can result in possessiveness in relationships, clinging tendencies, and a persistent need for reassurance. For friends and lovers, this intensity can be oppressive, resulting in a push-pull dynamic.

• ***Manipulation and Threats:*** People with BPD can use manipulation or threats to exert control over others and keep them from leaving. This conduct often backfires, alienating loved ones and bringing about the very result they are afraid of.

• ***Excessive Need for acceptance:*** The underlying fear of rejection or abandonment is the source of the continual need for validation and acceptance. This can result in people-pleasing actions that compromise personal needs to keep relationships intact.

It's critical to realize that this dread of being abandoned isn't caused by a lack of affection or concern. It's a pervasive worry that often has its origins in early instances of abandonment or loss.

Criteria 2: An Unsteady and Stressful Interpersonal Relationship Pattern

A person with BPD can have turbulent relationships that are marked by strong emotions and abrupt changes. The following difficulties are highlighted by this criterion:

• ***Ideation and Devaluation:*** Individuals with borderline personality disorder (BPD) can idealize a new acquaintance, therapist, or spouse because they think they are flawless and the solution to all of their issues. However, if the individual falls short of their irrational expectations or exhibits any apparent indication of disapproval, this strong idealization can soon turn into devaluation. This "splitting" tendency can cause pain and confusion for loved ones.

• ***Stormy Breakups and Difficulty Resolving disagreement:*** Because of the emotional instability linked to borderline personality disorder (BPD), managing disagreement in relationships can be difficult. Small disputes can become heated fights very fast. Furthermore, people with BPD can avoid disagreement entirely out of fear of being abandoned, which breeds anger and detachment.

• ***Irrational Expectations and the Need for Extreme Intimacy:*** Excessive need for connection might give rise to irrational expectations of intimate intimacy. As a result, friendships and romantic relationships can suffer since it can be difficult to sustain the intensity that a person with BPD craves.

Criteria 3: Identity Disturbance: Significantly and Continuously Unstable Self-Perception or Self-Image

Imagine attempting to construct a home on a sand foundation that keeps moving. BPD sufferers can experience something similar as they struggle with a continuously changing sense of who they are. This identity disorder can appear in several ways:

• *Chronic Sense of Emptiness:* BPD can be characterized by a persistent feeling of emptiness or a loss of meaning and purpose. This hole might encourage impetuous actions or frantic efforts to fill it with experiences or approval from others.

• *Regular Shifts in Values, Objectives, or Looks:* The pursuit of a steady self-image can result in regular shifts in one's looks, professional choices, or even worldviews. This can cause bewilderment for close ones and reinforce the person's sense of transience in life.

• *Doubts Regarding Morals and Core Values:* A lack of a strong sense of self can also affect morality and core values. This can result in trouble making judgments or a sense of being lost without a sense of direction from the inside.

Criteria 4: Impulsivity in a Minimum of Two Potentially Self-Destructive Areas

For many people with BPD, acting without thinking through the repercussions is a major difficulty. This impulsivity can show itself in several ways, often as a coping mechanism for strong emotions or a sense of emptiness:

• *Substance Abuse:* Using drugs or alcohol as a coping method for intense emotions might lead to self-medication. Substance misuse, however, can worsen psychological issues and bring on new difficulties in life.

• *Careless Spending and Gambling:* Risky gambling or impulsive shopping might operate as a momentary diversion from mental anguish. But these actions might have serious financial repercussions that add to the stress.

• *Unsafe Sexual Behavior:* Seeking affirmation or connection via several sexual partners or unprotected sex can be considered unsafe sexual behavior. On the other hand, this conduct can expose people to the danger of unintended pregnancy or STDs.

• ***Binge Eating:*** Eating a lot of food quickly, often without feeling hungry, might be a coping mechanism for emotional suffering or a technique to deal with feelings of emptiness. Weight gain and other health issues can result from this.

• ***Self-Harm:*** Cutting, burning, or beating oneself are examples of non-suicidal self-harm that can be used as a coping mechanism for intense feelings or as a tangible means to communicate emotional suffering. It's not a suicide attempt, but it can be a risky coping method and a cry for assistance.

It's important to realize that being impulsive does not indicate a lack of self-control. When someone has borderline personality disorder (BPD), their emotions might be so intense that they act without thinking through the repercussions to get relief right away.

Criteria 5: Repeated Acts of Suicide, Threats, or Self-Mutilating Behavior

Suicidal ideas, threats, and actions can result from the emotional turbulence associated with borderline personality disorder (BPD), especially in times of crisis or severe emotional distress. As was already noted, self-mutilating activities also meet this need. Let's take a deeper look:

• ***Suicidal Ideation and Attempts:*** For a person with BPD, suicide can be a desperate effort to end emotional suffering or a cry for assistance rather than a wish to die. It is important to take these concerns seriously and to get treatment right away.

• ***Self-Harm as a Coping Mechanism:*** Non-suicidal self-harm, as opposed to suicide attempts, can be a coping mechanism for intense emotions, a tangible means to convey emotional suffering, or a way to feel something while feeling emotionally detached. That being said, it's a risky coping strategy that needs help.

Criterion 6: Affective Instability and Marked Reactivity to Environmental Situations

Imagine if every little change in the surroundings caused an emotional barometer to fluctuate uncontrollably. This sums up emotional instability, a defining characteristic of borderline personality disorder. Feelings can change drastically and suddenly, ranging from extreme joy to debilitating melancholy. Here's a deeper examination of this requirement:

• ***Mood Swings:*** People with BPD can experience tremendous joy, rage, sorrow, or worry in brief bursts of time. Mood swings can be frequent and powerful. Both the person experiencing them and others around them can find these abrupt emotional changes to be disconcerting.

• *Hair-Trigger Reactivity:* Unexpected changes in plans, little occurrences, or even slights can elicit exaggerated emotional reactions. It can become difficult to handle commonplace circumstances and sustain wholesome connections as a result.

• *Difficulty Recovering from Emotional Upset:* BPD is known for its intense emotional state, which can make it challenging to "bounce back" from unpleasant feelings. People can find it difficult to revert to their initial emotional state after a failure or disappointment.

Those who are close to someone with BPD themselves need to comprehend this criterion. People can better handle these emotional swings by adopting healthy coping strategies and using emotional regulation techniques.

Criteria 7: Persistent Sense of Being Alone

This emptiness is more than just a lack of activities or boredom. It's an all-encompassing feeling of emptiness, of having a hole in the middle of oneself. Imagine looking out into an infinite void from the brink of a massive chasm. The essence of persistent emptiness in BPD is encapsulated in this vivid vision.

BPD patients can sense emptiness in many ways, including:

• *A Lack of Meaning and Purpose:* People with borderline personality disorder can have trouble finding meaning or purpose in life. They can wonder why they are here at all, feeling as if they are just existing in a vacuum. This lack of direction might exacerbate depressing and gloomy sentiments.

• *A Constant Yearning for Connection:* Another way that the emptiness could appear is as an ache for connection. This strong need for intimacy might result in clinging actions or frantic efforts to get experiences or approval from others to fill the vacuum. But they are often band-aid solutions, without addressing the fundamental emptiness.

• *Emotional Numbness:* The emptiness sometimes appears as an emotional numbness. People can feel emotionally cut off from others and unable to feel the same level of happiness, sorrow, or rage. This emotional numbness can be a coping method used to prevent the intense emotional agony brought on by the emptiness.

• *Identity Confusion:* A shaky or hazy sense of self might be linked to feelings of emptiness. People suffering from Borderline Personality Disorder can find it difficult to identify their identity, values, or areas of interest. This sense of emptiness can be made worse by this absence of a strong sense of self.

The persistent emptiness that BPD sufferers perceive might start a vicious cycle. This is how it transpires:

• *The Need to Escape the Void:* People with BPD can act impulsively to get away from the profound discomfort that comes with emptiness. Substance misuse, careless spending, unsafe sexual activity, or binge eating are some ways that this might show up. Although these actions can provide short-term comfort, they often have unfavorable effects that lead to further issues.

• *The Illusion of Filling the Void:* Impulsive activities might give rise to a transient "high" that gives the impression that the emptiness is being filled. But this is a transient state, and eventually, the emptiness returns, sometimes accompanied by regret, remorse, or humiliation.

• *The Deepening of the Void:* The cycle of impetuous actions and unfavorable outcomes might cause the emptiness to become deeper over time. People can have a sense of failure, which exacerbates the emptiness they are so frantically trying to fill and feeds their poor self-image.

Criteria 8: Improper, Severe Anger or Inability to Control Anger

Anger is a common emotion among people. Anger, however, can be a constant and overpowering emotion for a person with BPD. The criteria look like this:

• *Frequent Displays of Temper:* BPD is known to be characterized by frequent outbursts of rage, which are often brought on by insignificant occurrences. Relationship problems and an atmosphere of unpredictability can result from this.

• *Chronic wrath:* Resentment and wrath can simmer under the surface, affecting relationships and general well-being. It can be draining for the person with this chronic rage as well as others around them.

• *Frequent violent Fights:* In severe situations, fury can show itself as violent altercations. This emphasizes how crucial it is to have constructive outlets for your anger.

The destructive fury that is often seen in people with BPD must be distinguished from healthy expressions of rage. People with BPD who get therapy can learn how to recognize their triggers, control their emotions, and aggressively express their anger.

Criteria 9: Severe dissociative symptoms or transient paranoia related to stress

This criterion explores the territory of warped perceptions and a disassociation from reality. Let's investigate these two encounters:

• ***Transient, Stress-Related Paranoia:*** People with Borderline Personality Disorder (BPD) can go through phases of paranoia, which are marked by distrust and suspicion of other people. These emotions are often fleeting and brought on by stressful circumstances. For instance, based on little evidence, a person with BPD can accuse their spouse of adultery.

• ***Severe Dissociative Symptoms:*** A dissociative state is characterized by a sense of separation from oneself and one's environment. It might seem like a sense of unreality about your surroundings or the sensation that you are seeing yourself from outside of your body. These bouts of dissociation can be terrifying and unsettling.

It's crucial to remember that not every person with BPD will exhibit these particular symptoms. Nonetheless, being aware of these sheds light on the difficulties that people with BPD might encounter. It's critical to get expert assistance while experiencing these symptoms.

It will become clear when we look more thoroughly at these criteria in subsequent chapters, but the more recent DSM-IV-TR only slightly modifies the definition of symptoms. The inclusion of the ninth criterion, which acknowledges infrequent, frightening bouts of psychosis, is the biggest modification. The four main regions that this constellation of nine symptoms falls into—and where therapy is focused—are as follows:

· Erratic mood (criteria 1, 6, 7, and 8)

· Criteria 4 and 5: Impulsivity and uncontrollable conduct

· Relationship psychopathology (qualities two and three)

· Perception and thinking distortions (criterion 9)

The biggest contributors to suicide risk are mood swings and impulsivity. Researchers from throughout the nation collaborated to conduct a long-term study that classified these defining characteristics into three groups. These researchers validated the DSM variables that define BPD by interviewing hundreds of patients, evaluating the criteria, and classifying the results. The resulting three-factor clusters are:

Relationships that are disturbed: Relationships that are disturbed include issues with both oneself and others. Relationship problems will inevitably follow identity disruption. People who have ongoing identity uncertainty often experience emotions of emptiness and meaninglessness. Dissociation from reality happens when the feeling of self completely vanishes.

Uncontrolled behavior: Uncontrolled behavior covers destructive impulsivity and self-destructive behavior.

Mood irregularity: This includes all of the other requirements. Mood instability often results in frustration and inappropriate outbursts of fury. These strong feelings make the person feel alone and abandoned and alienate others.

A person is classified as having BPD if they meet at least five of the DSM criteria, or as not meeting the criteria if they have four or fewer symptoms. This approach makes room for quantifiable, objective factors. Nonetheless, it recognizes that each of the nine requirements plays an equal role in the disorder and permits the seemingly paradoxical possibility that an individual with a long-term BPD diagnosis can be "cured" of the condition by meeting only one criterion. On the other hand, other writers contend that personality disorders need to be defined dimensionally since they are persistent characteristics. According to this paradigm, personality functioning can be classified into degrees, just as addiction can be classified into different levels.

These writers contend that rather than concluding that a person is borderline or not, the condition should be identified along a spectrum based on the severity of symptoms shown and by weighing certain criteria and background data proportionally. Consider, for instance, that a person's male or female identity is categorical and objectively determined by several factors. On the other hand, labels of masculinity or femininity are subjective judgments based on cultural, personal, and other subjective standards. The use of dimensional models to redefine personality disorders (Axis II) is one of the proposals for the next DSM-V.

Now that you have examined the diagnostic criteria and dispelled common myths about BPD, you are well informed. But how BPD impacts day-to-day situations is where its real effects are seen. We'll focus on how BPD manifests in daily life in the next chapter, ***"The BPD Experience: Recognizing Manifestations."*** We'll look at the ups and downs in emotions, the difficulties in establishing and sustaining relationships, the occurrence of impulsive acts, and the never-ending quest for a solid sense of self. By being aware of these expressions, we can develop empathy, spot possible BPD symptoms, and eventually clear the door for appropriate assistance. Our ability to build a more rewarding life for ourselves and the people around us is enhanced by this greater awareness.

CHAPTER 2

The BPD Experience: Recognizing Types And Manifestations

In the last chapter, we established the foundation for understanding Borderline Personality Disorder. We investigated the diagnostic criteria used to diagnose BPD, distinguished it from prevalent myths and misunderstandings, and developed a broad understanding of the disorder. Now, we'll go further into the lived experience of BPD.

This chapter, "The BPD Experience: Recognizing Manifestations," takes us on a trip to see BPD firsthand. We'll look at how the main symptoms, the diagnostic criteria we covered before, transform into specific experiences. We'll look at the mental anguish, relational difficulties, urges that can lead to self-harm, and the fight with a fluctuating sense of identity. Recognizing these expressions allows us to use two strong tools: empathy and awareness. We can have a better understanding of the difficulties experienced by those with BPD, promoting compassion and support. Perhaps more crucially, this understanding can assist us in identifying indicators of BPD in others and, perhaps, inside ourselves.

Previously, individuals could have considered Borderline Personality Disorder (BPD) as a straightforward disorder with a few symptoms. But it isn't the complete picture. As a therapist who has dealt with many clients with BPD for years, I've seen how this disorder manifests itself in a variety of ways. It's similar to putting together a jigsaw with numerous parts, yet each puzzle is unique. Understanding the many manifestations of BPD allows us to go beyond a simple diagnosis and develop more effective treatment approaches for each person.

Here, we'll look at seven key areas where BPD might manifest in a person's life:

1. Emotional sensitivity

Borderline Personality Disorder (BPD) is a complicated illness with a variety of issues. One of the most important and influential characteristics is emotional sensitivity. This does not merely suggest experiencing emotions more profoundly; it refers to the overpowering intensity, unexpected frequency, and quick fluctuations in emotions, which can be very difficult to control.

Mood swings.

Some people with BPD have frequent and strong mood fluctuations as a result of their emotional sensitivity. Consider how moments of pure bliss can suddenly transform into crushing grief, apparently out of nowhere. Anger can soar from zero to one hundred in an instant, driven by apparently little incidents. This emotional instability can be quite disconcerting. You can find yourself unable to foresee or comprehend your emotions, leaving you feeling confused and overwhelmed. The environment around you might seem uncertain and hazardous, matching the erratic character of your own emotions.

Others with BPD can have a persistent undercurrent of intense emotions. Imagine a pot of water simmering on the stove, always on the edge of boiling over. This constantly boiling pot signifies a heightened emotional state. It's a state of emotional arousal that can be taxing, depleting your energy reserves and making it difficult to concentrate on everyday chores or negotiate social situations. You can feel on edge, continuously awaiting the release of powerful emotions that might be expressed as emotional outbursts or withdrawal. The persistent state of hypervigilance can be very stressful and alienating.

The Impact on Relationships

Emotional sensitivity in BPD can have a substantial influence on your capacity to form and maintain healthy relationships. Those close to you can find your emotions puzzling and even terrifying due to their intensity and unpredictability. Imagine attempting to manage a relationship when your emotional compass seems to be constantly spinning. Building trust and managing the complexity of relationships can be an ongoing discussion, leaving you feeling uneasy and misunderstood.

But there is hope. Understanding your emotional sensitivity and how it affects your life can allow you to begin developing skills and strategies for regulating your emotions and cultivating better relationships. Here are the first stages on this path of self-discovery and empowerment:

Mindfulness Techniques: Recognizing the early indicators of emotional dysregulation is critical. This entails paying great attention to your physical feelings. Are your muscles tense? Is your heartbeat racing? Consider your thoughts: are you using negative self-talk or catastrophizing? Identify your emotional urges: do you have a strong want to isolate yourself or strike out verbally? By being more aware of your internal condition, you can learn to predict emotional outbursts and intervene before they worsen.

Emotion Regulation Skills: Learning healthy coping techniques is critical for effectively managing high emotions. Deep breathing techniques might assist relax your nervous system in the moment. Progressive muscular relaxation can assist relieve physical strain caused by emotional excitement. Journaling can help you express and manage tough emotions safely and healthily. Investigate several strategies to see what works best for you.

Communication Strategies: Improving your communication skills will help you express your feelings more effectively and create trust in relationships. Assertiveness training can be very useful in learning to articulate your requirements clearly and effectively, without resorting to anger or manipulation. Tell people closest to you what emotional support looks like for you. Open and honest communication is essential for developing strong and healthy relationships.

Seeking Professional Support: If you are suffering, receiving professional support from a therapist who specializes in BPD therapy can be quite beneficial. A therapist can provide specialized direction and support, assisting you in developing a complete treatment plan that suits your unique requirements. They can also teach you more skills for dealing with emotional dysregulation and developing healthy relationships.

2. Needing Connection and Fearing Abandonment: Relationship Challenges

Borderline Personality Disorder (BPD) creates particular problems for developing and sustaining healthy relationships. One of the most common difficulties is a deep fear of abandonment or being left alone. This dread might emerge in apparently contradictory ways, influencing how you interact with people.

The dread of abandonment is a distinguishing feature of Borderline Personality Disorder. It's more than just a passing anxiety; it's a continual, nagging fear that someone you care about can abandon you, irreversibly changing the course of your life. This dread goes beyond romantic relationships and includes family members, friends, and even strangers.

The fear of desertion might be imagined or actual, blurring the distinction between a reasonable worry and a strong emotional reaction.

Hypervigilance and misinterpretations

Individuals with BPD often exhibit heightened sensitivity to perceived slights. A benign activity, such as a family member moving items in the garage, might be misconstrued as a clear indication of approaching desertion. This misconception can cause a chain reaction of negative feelings, causing the person with BPD to fear that their whole family is going to vanish. Similarly, a tiny disagreement with a spouse might be misinterpreted as the beginning of a separation, throwing the relationship into disarray. This continual state of hypervigilance can be very stressful, not just for the individual with BPD, but also for their loved ones.

The Push-and-Pull cycle

Individuals with BPD can engage in the "push-and-pull" dynamic to assert control over this imagined danger. This is intentionally pushing loved ones away to prevent the expected agony of abandonment. This conduct can be very perplexing and emotionally taxing for individuals on the receiving end. Imagine repeatedly being accused of abandoning someone who needs your help; it's no wonder that some relationships fail under such pressure. The pain of a true breakup therefore reinforces the same fear the person with BPD was attempting to avoid, resulting in a self-fulfilling prophesy.

The Roots of Fear: Exploring Childhood Experiences

The origins of this strong dread of abandonment are often planted in childhood trauma. Here are a few critical variables that might help it develop:

• *Losing a parent, foster parent, or caregiver can be very distressing.* This can involve cases of neglect, abuse, or even homelessness.

• *Emotional Neglect or Abuse:* Unmet emotional needs can lead to feelings of abandonment, even without physical separation. This can be caused by emotionally distant caregivers or those who display scary or unexpected actions for children.

• *Family instability:* Inconsistent parental attachment can cause worry for children. Inconsistency, whether deliberate or accidental, can make it harder for a kid to form strong and healthy attachments, affecting future relationships.

The Deep Scars of Trauma

Perceived desertion, whether physical or mental, can have long-term consequences for a kid. These events can be very difficult to absorb at such a young age, yet the memories persist as a continual reminder of vulnerability. When these memories are aroused, a person can have an overpowering sense that they are doomed to be abandoned again. This anxiety becomes so firmly established in their brain that it alters their view of current relationships, making it difficult to trust and connect with others.

Need for Connection and Fear of Rejection

Some people with BPD, anxious to prevent abandonment, can create very deep bonds quickly. This strong need for connection can cause you to rely significantly on partners or friends for emotional support, perhaps becoming too reliant. While this initial intimacy can seem comforting, it can become overpowering for loved ones, resulting in an unhealthy dynamic in the relationship. Alternatively, fear of rejection and betrayal can lead to social isolation. You can find yourself avoiding intimacy completely, unable to create enduring ties. This isolation can intensify emotions of loneliness and emptiness, adding to the dread of abandonment.

Understanding impulsive behaviors

BPD patients' high emotions can often lead to impulsive acts as a coping mechanism for emotional discomfort. These activities can seem chaotic or irresponsible, but it is critical to recognize that they are not spontaneous outbursts. Instead, they represent a desperate effort to deal with enormous emotional suffering. Imagine yourself stuck in a rip current, tossed and twisted by strong emotions. You can be inclined to resist the river, exerting all of your energy with minimal results. Impulsive actions in BPD can be like clutching onto anything that can provide momentary relief, even if it comes with its own set of hazards.

High-risk choices

High-risk decisions are a prevalent sign of emotional dysregulation in BPD. These can include a wide range of behaviors, such as drug misuse, irresponsible spending, and dangerous sexual conduct. It is critical to recognize that these activities, although damaging, often function as a temporary coping method for people with BPD.

Several underlying demands can lead to these high-risk decisions:

• *Escape Emotional Pain:* BPD can cause overpowering feelings. Substance misuse, for example, might provide a short-term numbing effect, allowing you to escape from emotional anguish.

• *BPD patients can fail to manage their emotions well*. High-risk habits can be a mistaken effort to handle overwhelming emotions, even if the respite is temporary.

• *Filling a void:* BPD sufferers can experience feelings of emptiness due to fear of abandonment. Risky activities can be a subconscious effort to fill this emptiness, even if they have harmful repercussions.

Consider Sarah (name altered for privacy), a 28-year-old woman diagnosed with BPD. Sarah suffered frequent mood swings between pleasure and devastating grief. When she was feeling low, she would experience enormous emptiness and a great dread of being alone. To cope, she would go on impulsive shopping sprees, purchasing costly clothing and accessories. While these purchases brought a brief rush of pleasure and joy, the financial burden eventually aggravated her mental misery. Sarah's tale demonstrates how high-risk decisions might be a maladaptive effort to cope with complicated emotions.

Self-harm and the Call for Help

Self-harm is a problematic symptom that can occur in people with BPD. It is critical to recognize that these actions are not efforts to terminate one's life, but rather a desperate cry for assistance, a method to express great emotional suffering or cope with overpowering sensations that seem difficult to endure.

The desire to self-harm might result from a complicated interaction of causes.

• *Emotional Release:* BPD can cause intense emotions that might be overwhelming. Self-harm, in its warped form, might provide a momentary relief from the overwhelming mental agony. The physical pain caused might serve as a diversion, offering a little respite from the mental turmoil inside. Consider Mark (name changed for privacy), a 22-year-old with BPD. Following a quarrel with his partner, Mark experienced a crushing feeling of emptiness and sadness. Unable to express his feelings, he sliced his arm. While the physical discomfort did not alleviate his mental distress, it did give a brief diversion, enabling him to dull the intensity of his emotions.

• *BPD patients typically fail to articulate their feelings effectively:* Self-harm can be a mistaken effort to convey inner suffering, or a technique to express grief when words fail. Sarah (name altered to preserve privacy) has BPD and suffers from strong abandonment concerns. When her closest friend cancels plans at the last minute, Sarah experiences a wave of anxiety and solitude. Unable to convey her dread of being alone vocally, she can turn to self-harm to express her inner agony and urgent desire for connection.

• ***BPD often leads to feelings of being out of control:*** Self-harm might provide a temporary sensation of control in an overwhelming and uncertain environment.

3. Finding Your Place: Identity Puzzle and Disturbance

Borderline Personality Disorder (BPD) poses a particular challenge to a basic human need: the need to know who we are. For the majority of individuals, this sense of self serves as a solid basis, directing their ideas, actions, and relationships. However, for those with BPD, this internal compass swings irregularly, causing a widespread identity disorder. Imagine waking up every day, uncertain of who you see in the mirror. Many people with BPD experience a continual state of questioning and flux. Internally, it's a never-ending search for answers, a need to establish a sense of self that seems forever out of grasp. The absence of a steady core can be very unsettling, making it difficult to navigate daily life.

External manifestations:

The emotional anguish of identity disorder often emerges in external actions. Here are a few such scenarios:

• ***Chameleon-like transformations:*** A frantic quest for self might result in significant alterations in appearance. Frequent hair color changes, abrupt adjustments in fashion style, and impulsive tattoos and piercings are all efforts to discover an outward expression of an elusive interior self.

• ***Shifting Identity:*** Uncertain about their basic beliefs and who they are, some people with BPD can mimic the qualities and interests of others around them to experience a feeling of belonging. This can result in a continually fluctuating sense of self, similar to a chameleon adjusting to its environment.

• ***Self-Definition:*** The Shifting Sands Some people with BPD can even alter their names in the hopes that a new identity would help them feel more confident about themselves.

• ***Emptiness or lack of direction:*** Others can have intense feelings of emptiness and a lack of direction in life. They can struggle to define their objectives, values, or long-term ambitions, creating a sense of being lost. A lack of a consistent sense of self might make it difficult to live a satisfying life.

The Causes of Identity Crisis: The scars of trauma

The road to self-discovery starts in infancy and is affected by our surroundings. When a kid encounters trauma, such as neglect, abuse, or an emotionally detached upbringing, the basis for a healthy identity is severely weakened. This trauma can appear in a variety of ways, affecting a child's confidence, assertiveness, and general self-esteem. Here's how trauma might impede the formation of a healthy identity:

• Shahida Arabi's study on children raised by narcissistic parents reveals the negative impact of "chronic gaslighting" (manipulation that causes individuals to doubt their sanity). This can result in an overwhelming feeling of self-doubt in maturity, making it difficult to trust one's observations and experiences. Building a healthy identity is difficult without a solid foundation of self-validation.

• *Embodied trauma:* Trauma can leave profound emotional scars that, if not treated, can become imprinted in a person's sense of identity. This can lead to a scenario in which someone feels like they are always reliving their terrible events, impeding the formation of a healthy, autonomous self.

People with BPD often struggle with a sense of self that is vague or confused. This can emerge in several ways:

Jon's Story: A Case of Lost Identity.

Jon, a guy with BPD, spoke with Project UROK about his issues with identification. He recounted continually modifying himself to match the mold of anybody he was interested in at the moment. This continuous desire for external affirmation resulted in a tragic realization: he lacked a true sense of self. This interior emptiness resulted in suicidal thoughts and hospitalization. Even after therapy, Jon struggled with the central question: "Who is Jon?" Jon's tale vividly depicts the terrible consequences of identity disorder. Without a strong sense of self, it is almost hard to treat the underlying causes of BPD and live a satisfying life.

Luckily, there is hope. Therapy can be an effective tool for those with BPD in navigating these problems. To address identity disturbances, people might use Cognitive Behavioral Therapy (CBT) to identify and confront problematic self-beliefs.

• ***Improve Emotional Regulation Skills:*** Learning healthy strategies to regulate high emotions might minimize the need for external validation or self-destructive habits to identify oneself.

• ***Foster a Strong Support System:*** Having a network of supporting loved ones can create a feeling of belonging and stability, resulting in a good self-image.

4. Black and White Thinking: Idealization and Devaluation.

One of the characteristics of BPD is a coping mechanism called "splitting," in which people see themselves and others in extremes of black and white - either perfectly excellent or irredeemably evil. This might show as passionately idealizing someone at first, putting them on a pedestal, and ignoring their imperfections. However, a perceived betrayal or slight might result in a fast devaluation, in which the individual is immediately seen as completely negative. This mistaken thinking habit can devastate relationships, resulting in a perpetual push-and-pull dynamic that leaves both parties feeling confused and emotionally exhausted.

Imagine meeting someone new and having an immediate connection so strong that it feels like returning home. Individuals with BPD often have this feeling when they meet someone, they believe is unique. This technique, known as idealization, is putting the other person on a pedestal, concentrating entirely on their good characteristics while ignoring any apparent shortcomings. They can perceive this person as their soulmate, the one who can finally fill the gap they've felt for so long. This intensive idealization fosters a strong relationship, yet it is based on erroneous expectations.

The frail house of cards built during idealization might shatter with the smallest perceived error. A missed phone call, a change in plans, or even a quarrel can all be viewed as betrayal, resulting in a sudden and dramatic shift in perspective. This devaluation entails perceiving the once-idealized person as completely negative, concentrating primarily on their defects and reducing or even deleting the favorable attributes formerly praised. The powerful feelings experienced during idealization might lead to wrath, dissatisfaction, and even hate.

The continual oscillation between idealization and depreciation results in a chaotic and unpredictable interpersonal dynamic. Here is how it plays out:

•   The first encounter might create unreasonable expectations and a passionate bond.

- As a relationship matures, arguments and disappointments are inevitable.

- Perceived slights or betrayals can lead to devaluation and the breakdown of an idealized image.

- BPD individuals can exhibit push-and-pull behavior, such as verbal outbursts or emotional withdrawal, which can distance them from others.

- The fear of desertion is a powerful motivator. Pushing someone away might help you escape the expected sorrow of being abandoned. The irony is that this conduct often drives the other person away, increasing the exact anxiety it was designed to guard against.

Breaking the Cycle: Towards Healthy Relationships

While this dynamic might be daunting, there is still potential for healthy partnerships. Here are several strategies to go forward:

- *Therapy can help persons with BPD identify and control splitting behaviors:* Individuals can learn to confront their erroneous thinking habits and manage relationships more effectively if they grasp the underlying reasons for this protective mechanism.

- *Developing Emotional Regulation Skills:* Managing strong emotions can avoid devaluation. Techniques such as mindfulness and communication skills training can be quite beneficial.

- *Strong self-esteem is crucial for developing healthy bonds*: Therapy can help persons with BPD create a positive self-image, lessening their need for external validation and the severe idealization that leads to devaluation.

5. Feeling Disconnected: Overwhelming Emotions.

Individuals with BPD often experience intense emotions, which can seem overpowering and all-consuming. This emotional instability can result in dissociation, a condition in which a person feels separated from themselves or their environment. This might emerge as a sense of disconnection from oneself or one's surroundings as if you were watching a movie of your life develop from a distance. Dissociation can also function as a coping technique, helping people to momentarily escape overwhelming emotions or uncomfortable events. However, prolonged dissociation can have a substantial influence on an individual's capacity to operate in everyday life.

Dissociation occurs on a continuum and manifests in a variety of ways:

• *Depersonalization*: feeling disconnected from oneself as if viewing one's thoughts, feelings, and behaviors from a distance. Imagine watching a movie about your own life and feeling strangely uninterested in the growing action.

• *Derealization:* refers to seeing reality as unreal, distorted, or dreamy. Familiar surroundings can look foggy or distant, and daily noises can become muted or distorted.

• *Out-of-Body Experiences:* In rare situations, people can feel as if their awareness has detached from their body and is gazing down from above.

Consider Sarah's story.

Sarah, a 23-year-old woman with BPD, recently had a furious altercation with her closest friend. The intensity of the emotions—anger, hurt, and fear of abandonment—is excruciating. Sarah now feels a weird separation. Her surroundings become fuzzy, and her body feels numb. She is still there in the scenario, but she is emotionally detached, taking shelter in a mental fog. While dissociation gives a momentary reprieve from emotional distress, it does not address the root causes.

The Risks of Chronic Dissociation

While dissociation can offer a brief relief from mental pain, ongoing dissociation can have significant negative effects. Here's how:

• *Impaired Daily Functioning:* Dissociation can make it difficult to focus on tasks, maintain relationships, or manage daily responsibilities. When you feel separated from yourself and the world around you, it's difficult to fully participate in life.

• *Missed Opportunities for Growth:* Dissociation can block people from understanding and learning from tough feelings. By ignoring the pain, they can miss chances for personal growth and mental healing.

• *Increased Risk of Self-Harm:* Dissociation can cause a sense of unreality, making self-harm more likely. If someone feels removed from the actual pain of self-harm, they can participate in more dangerous behaviors.

Finding Solid Ground: Breaking the Cycle of Dissociation

Fortunately, there are methods to handle detachment and promote mental well-being. Here are some ways forward:

Mindfulness Techniques: Learning to be present in the moment can help individuals become more aware of dissociation as it's happening. Techniques like meditation and deep breathing exercises can be useful tools.

Grounding methods: When separation happens, grounding methods can help people reunite with their bodies and surroundings. This could involve focusing on the five senses, such as feeling the texture of an item or taking deep breaths and noticing the rise and fall of your chest.

6. Chronic Anger and Frustration

One of the features of BPD is emotional intensity, and for some people, this appears as a steady background of anger and frustration. Imagine a pot of water bubbling on the stove, constantly on the edge of boiling over. This boiling pot is a metaphor for the experience of many with BPD – a low-grade anger that can explode into outbursts or more subtle, passive-aggressive behaviors.

Hair-Trigger Irritability: When Minor Annoyances Spark Rage

Daily life can feel like a trap for someone with ongoing anger and rage. Imagine feeling like you're constantly walking on eggshells, worried that the slightest thing – a perceived look, a missed compliment, a change in plans, a minor inconvenience – a long line at the grocery store, a delayed train, or a perceived slight from a colleague – can trigger an outpouring of anger that seems disproportionate to the situation. This is the truth for many with BPD. Their emotional sensitivity is turned up too high, making them prone to strong responses that can seem disproportionate to the situation. This anger can make it difficult to keep mental control and handle everyday encounters.

While outbursts are certainly a possibility, ongoing anger in BPD can appear in more delicate ways as well:

• ***Passive-Aggressive Behavior:*** Giving someone the quiet treatment, backhanded praise, or deliberately doing the opposite of what someone asks can be ways of showing anger subtly. While these behaviors can seem less aggressive, they can be just as damaging to relationships.

- ***Self-Directed Anger:*** Sometimes, the anger goes inward, leading to self-criticism, self-blame, and even self-harm. This inner anger can be just as damaging as open shows.

- ***Verbal Barrage:*** A flood of angry words, charges, and hurtful insults can explode, leaving those around feeling confused, hurt, and afraid.

- ***Physical Actions:*** In some cases, anger can turn physical, with items being thrown, doors being slammed, or even aggressive behavior aimed at others.

While these shows of anger can seem aggressive, it's important to understand the deeper feelings at play. Often, the anger comes from a primal fear of loss. Individuals with BPD can see anger as a way to protect themselves from imagined threats, a way to regain a sense of control in a situation that feels overwhelming.

However, the wake of an explosion is often filled with sorrow and shame. The person with BPD can feel embarrassed by their behavior and afraid that their loved ones will leave them. This fear of loss can then cause a loop of self-destructive behaviors, such as self-harm or suicide thoughts, as a desperate attempt to reconnect with those they've pushed away.

Exploring the Roots: The Seeds of Anger Sown in Trauma

To understand ongoing anger in BPD, it's important to consider the possible root reasons. Here are some things that can contribute:

- ***Emotional Dysregulation:*** Individuals with BPD often struggle to control their feelings successfully. This means that even small complaints can quickly grow into extreme anger.

- ***Fear of Abandonment:*** A core fear in BPD is the fear of being abandoned by loved ones. This fear can make people hypervigilant about any imagined risks, leading to anger as a pre-emptive defense strategy.

- ***Childhood Trauma:*** Experiences of neglect, abuse, or invalidation in childhood can have a lifelong effect on mental growth. Children who grow up in these settings can never learn good ways to handle anger, leading to ongoing frustration in adulthood.

A Case of Misunderstood Frustration: The Story of Daniel

Daniel, a 28-year-old man with BPD, constantly feels like he's on edge. The world seems full of annoyances – slow drivers, noisy neighbors, and coworkers who don't meet schedules. These daily complaints quickly build into a bubbling anger that affects his interactions. He can snap at his partner over small things or withdraw mentally, leaving her feeling confused and hurt. Daniel doesn't understand why he gets so angry, and his outbursts often push loved ones away, confirming the very fear of loss that fuels his anger in the first place.

Sammy-Marie's Story: A Life Shaped by Trauma

Sammy-Marie, who fought with BPD after a difficult childhood, described her anger as once uncontrolled. She spoke of frequent fights during her school years and explosive outbursts in a past relationship. These seemingly random shows of rage were, in fact, a constant internal fight. The emotional instability caused by her trauma left her without the tools to control her anger healthily.

How To Break the Cycle

Fortunately, there are ways to handle ongoing anger and frustration in BPD. Here are some steps toward mental well-being:

• *Therapy:* A therapist can help people with BPD explore the root reasons for their anger and create healthy coping strategies. Techniques like awareness training and mood control routines can be useful tools.

• *Identifying Triggers:* By learning to identify events or actions that cause their anger, people can develop methods to avoid or control those triggers more effectively.

• Communication Skills Training: Learning to communicate needs and feelings clearly and assertively can help prevent misunderstandings and reduce the likelihood of emotional outbursts.

• Building a Support System: Having a network of supportive loved ones who understand BPD can provide a safe space for expressing emotions and navigating difficult situations.

• With self-awareness, commitment to therapy, and a supportive network, individuals with BPD can learn to manage their anger and frustration healthily, building more fulfilling relationships and a calmer inner world.

7. Chronic Feelings of Failure, Emptiness, and Self-Criticism: A Harsh Inner Critic

Many people with BPD deal with a tough inner critic. This can appear as a constant stream of self-criticism and feelings of failure. Even small losses or imagined mistakes can cause deep shame and self-blame. This bad self-image can add to feelings of sadness and make it difficult for people to build self-compassion and self-acceptance. Learning to question these negative thoughts and develop a more healthy self-perception is an important part of care for BPD.

One of the features of BPD is a persistent sense of failure and self-doubt, often driven by a merciless inner critic. Imagine living with a constant voice in your head, a voice that constantly criticizes your every move, magnifies your flaws, and diminishes your achievements. This, sadly, is the truth for many people with BPD.

The Sting of Shame: From Minor Setbacks to Major Meltdowns

Even the most small failure can cause a flood of negativity within someone dealing with a harsh inner critic. A missed goal at work, a critical word from a friend, or even an imagined social faux pas can grow into strong feelings of shame and self-blame. This skewed self-perception can make it difficult to manage a normal life without feeling like a constant failure.

The tough inner reviewer doesn't just speak in words. It can appear in different ways:

• *All-or-Nothing Thinking:* The inner reviewer can view things in extremes. A good performance at work is never good enough, social contact is deemed a complete disaster if it's not perfect, and any imagined mistake is seen as a catastrophic failure.

• *Negative Self-Talk: A* steady flood of negative thoughts about oneself bombards the individual, eating away at their self-esteem and sense of worth. Phrases like "I'm worthless," "I'm a failure," and "Nobody loves me" become a familiar and damaging story.

• *Social Comparison Traps:* The inner reviewer can constantly compare the individual to others, showing perceived flaws and increasing weaknesses. This social comparison can lead to feelings of failure and envy.

The Empty Void: Disconnection from the Self

The constant negative from the inner reviewer can add to a deep sense of nothingness. When an individual constantly feels weak and unworthy, it becomes difficult to connect with their true self. They can feel like they are merely a collection of flaws and mistakes, unable to experience real happiness or satisfaction.

As a therapist focusing on Borderline Personality Disorder (BPD), I see the fight with emptiness directly. Many of my clients describe a deep hollowness within, a sense of living yet missing a core sense of self. It's a paradox – feelings can feel overwhelming at times, yet there's also a deep silence. This emptiness can create a strong desire for connection, a longing to fill the gap with something, anything, external to oneself. Relationships become a refuge, giving a brief sense of health. However, these links are often filled with uncertainty. The fear of rejection, a feature of BPD, can lead to obsessive behaviors or strong emotional dependence.

In the lack of healthy coping strategies, some individuals with BPD can turn to rash actions to numb the emptiness. Substance abuse, careless spending, or self-harm might provide a brief sense of comfort, but eventually leave them feeling even more hollow. These distractions are like putting a patch on a broken leg – they handle the instant pain but don't fix the core problem. It's important to understand that this silence often stems from childhood events. If you grew up in a damaging setting where your feelings and needs were ignored or belittled, you can have learned to separate from your true self. This can have a permanent effect on your sense of self-worth.

The key to beating this nothingness lies in building a strong internal source of self-worth. Unlike non-sufferers who can find satisfaction mentally, people with BPD often deal with this idea. Therapy can be a useful tool in this process. Here are some methods we can explore together:

A Case of Crushing Self-Doubt: The Story of Mary

Mary, a 25-year-old artist with BPD, constantly feels like a fake. Despite her obvious ability, any time she gets praise for her work, the inner reviewer says, "They're just being nice. You're not good." A bad day in the studio can cause a slide of self-doubt, leading her to think she has no artistic ability whatsoever. This tough self-criticism leaves her feeling emotionally tired and removed from her drive. The joy of making art, once a source of great pleasure, becomes soured by the constant criticism.

Quieting the Critic

Fortunately, there are ways to challenge the tough inner reviewer and develop a more positive self-image. Here are some steps towards mental well-being:

Cognitive Behavioral Therapy (CBT): CBT can be a strong tool in helping people with BPD spot and question negative thought habits that lead to feelings of sadness. By learning to notice and change skewed thinking, people can begin to create a more balanced and caring self-view.

Mindfulness Practices: Mindfulness exercises can help people become more aware of their inner critic and learn to separate from its negative. By watching their thoughts without judgment, people can begin to disidentify with the harsh self-talk and build a more objective view of themselves. By becoming more aware of your thoughts and feelings, you can begin to understand the sadness and build better ways to handle it.

Developing Self-Compassion: Learning to treat oneself with kindness and understanding is vital in beating the harsh inner critic. Practicing self-compassion involves admitting one's flaws while also recognizing one's strengths and successes. We can explore your ideals, hobbies, and skills. Building self-awareness and a feeling of personal identity is crucial in creating a basis of self-worth, regardless of outward support.

The good news is that healing is possible. Therapy can provide a safe space to explore the emotional scars of your past and create better ways of connecting to yourself and others. By learning to support your inner self and build a strong sense of self-worth, you can begin to fill the void with something more solid – self-compassion, self-acceptance, and a real sense of health.

The 4 Types of Borderline Personality Disorder

There are four main types of BPD. It is important to understand the differences between them as the appearance of BPD can reveal the underlying thought patterns, and this will impact how each individual's BPD treatment should be focused.

1. Impulsive Borderline Personality Disorder

Impulsive Borderline Personality Disorder (BPD) presents a unique problem. As the name suggests, impulsivity takes center stage, showing in a variety of risky and possibly dangerous behaviors. Yet, beneath this volatile surface often lies a fascinating energy and charm that can be both appealing and puzzling. People with reckless BPD can be incredibly interesting. Imagine the life of the party, quick with a smart comment and having an undeniable magnetism. This charm can draw others in, creating a feeling of joy and adventure. However, beneath this surface lies a deeper fight for control and a widespread fear of rejection. This fear can appear in seemingly opposite ways:

• ***Elusive Intimacy:*** Despite their social nature, individuals with reckless BPD can keep a certain emotional space. This "push-pull" relationship can be confusing to others. They can crave closeness yet fight to fully commit, fearing the potential for rejection.

• ***The Allure of Attention:*** Flirting can become a tool for finding approval and a sense of control. They can crave attention, sometimes even playing improperly, without necessarily having a real love interest.

• ***The Allure of Drama:*** Attention-seeking habits can appear in various ways, from causing pointless drama to acting recklessly. This can be a desperate attempt to ensure they stay the center of attention, a way to manage their inner fear of being ignored or forgotten. The reckless nature of this subtype often leads to a life spent on the edge. These actions can serve multiple goals, from handling overwhelming feelings to exerting control

• ***Substance Abuse:*** Substance abuse, whether booze, drugs, or other substances, can provide a brief escape from the mental chaos within. However, this road often leads to addiction and further complicates their lives.

• ***Reckless Activities:*** Reckless activities, from driving under the influence to participating in unsafe sex, can become a way to seek excitement and feel a sense of power. The thrill of the moment often trumps any thought of long-term effects.

• ***Impulsive Spending Sprees:*** The desire to fill a gap or feel a sense of power can lead to careless spending sprees, leaving them in financial trouble. These binges can be a brief attempt to soothe a deeper sense of emptiness.

• ***Volatile Relationships:*** Their strong need for control and fear of loss can cause chaotic and uncertain partnerships. They can be protective, jealous, and prone to emotional tantrums, pushing loved ones away.

It's crucial to understand that reckless BPD often comes from a childhood marked by neglect, abuse, or invalidation. If a child's basic needs for love, security, and approval are not met, they can develop a deep sense of nothingness and a skewed sense of self. This can lead to a steady desire for outward praise and a problem controlling feelings in a healthy way. They can never have formed a strong sense of self-worth, leaving them open to influence and badly wanting approval from others.

This deep-seated need for approval can cause a deadly loop. Their rash behaviors can be a hopeless attempt to gain control of their relationships or feel a sense of power over their own lives. Here's how this cycle often unfolds:

• *Risky Behavior for Attention:* They engage in reckless acts to gain the approval or recognition of others, hoping to feel a sense of control and avoid criticism.

• *Negative Consequences:* The rash behavior often leads to negative consequences, such as financial loss, broken relationships, or legal trouble.

• *Deeper Emptiness:* These results can further support the feeling of emptiness and lack of control, leading them back to seeking approval through more rash actions.

2. Discouraged Borderline Personality Disorder

Discouraged Borderline Personality Disorder (DBPD), often referred to as "quiet BPD," offers a unique set of problems. Unlike the more openly explosive forms of BPD, people with DBPD tend to internalize their problems, making identification and assistance more complicated. Yet, beneath the seemingly calm surface lies a potent storm of feelings – a deep-seated fear of loss and a constant desire for connection.

The Mask of Perfection: A Facade of Success

People with DBPD can look to have it all together. They might be high achievers, pushed by a dogged chase of greatness. This perfectionism can appear in various areas of their lives – jobs, studies, and relationships – creating an image of success and control. However, this facade often hides a deep sense of failure and a constant fight for self-worth.

The Paradox of Connection: Yearning Yet Detached

Despite their outward success, people with DBPD often feel deeply separated and detached from others. They crave praise and acceptance yet hold a deep suspicion of closeness, fearing the potential for rejection. This fear can lead to self-isolating behaviors, creating a painful paradox – desperately wanting interaction while simultaneously pushing it away.

Clinging On vs. Pushing Away

The fear of loss can appear in seemingly contrary behaviors. On the one hand, people with DBPD can show "clingy" or codependent behaviors, badly wanting constant reinforcement and approval from others. This can put a strain on relationships, as it can feel overwhelming to the other person. On the other hand, fearing this very dependence, they can suddenly withdraw, pushing loved ones away before they can be the ones to start the loss they dread. Hidden beneath the surface often lies a turbulent inner world. While they can appear to calm outwardly, people with DBPD can experience strong and quickly changing feelings. The fear of loss can cause excessive anger, frustration, and hopelessness. However, unlike some other BPD subtypes, they often turn this pessimism inwards, participating in self-blame and self-criticism. This can lead to self-harming habits as a way to cope with the mental chaos within.

The Roots of Discouraged BPD

Discouraged BPD often stems from a background of childhood abuse or mental mistreatment. These events can have a long-term effect on a person's sense of self-worth and ability to trust others. If a child's basic wants for love, protection, and approval are not met, they can develop an inner belief that they are unlovable or worthless. This negative self-image feeds the endless comparison to others and the constant fear of rejection.

3. Petulant Borderline Personality Disorder (PBPD)

Petulant Borderline Personality Disorder (PBPD) presents a unique set of problems for those labeled with it and the people in their lives. Individuals with PBPD experience an explosive mix of feelings, marked by random and dramatic mood swings. This emotional instability can be incredibly damaging to their daily functioning and relationships.

Unpredictable Mood Shifts

The hallmark trait of PBPD is the fast and strong change of mood. Imagine a sunny day suddenly changing into a violent rainstorm – that's the mental scene for someone with PBPD. One moment they might be laughing wildly, sharing lighthearted jokes, and the next they erupt in a fiery rage or sink into a pit of misery, often triggered by seemingly unimportant events. A perceived slight, a missed phone call, or a change in plans can be the spark that starts an emotional explosion. This emotional instability is incredibly upsetting for those who deal with them. Loved ones can never quite guess what might set them off, causing a constant sense of walking on eggshells.

A Fragile Core Beneath the Anger

These strong emotional shows often hide a deeper weakness. Individuals with PBPD can fight with a deep sense of fear and a core belief that they are unworthy of love and support. When their needs are not met, or they perceive a slight, this fear can appear as a flood of anger, frustration, and bitterness. This anger can be a defense strategy, a way of pushing people away before they experience the feared sting of rejection. It's a desperate attempt to protect themselves from further mental pain.

Challenges in Relationships

Relationships can be a complicated and hard area for people with PBPD. Their extreme possessiveness and need for control can be suffocating to partners. They can show deceptive behaviors, trying to control the scenario and ensure their wants are met. This trickery can breed animosity and weaken trust within the relationship. Furthermore, their stubbornness and trouble accepting fault can make conflict settlement a nearly impossible job. However, despite these difficulties, people with PBPD can be extremely loyal and loving partners when they feel safe and supported.

Understanding the Roots

The roots of PBPD can often be linked back to childhood stress. Experiences of rejection, neglect, or mental abuse can have a long effect on a person's sense of self-worth and ability to trust others. Children who experience these tragedies can develop a hypervigilance to any imagined threat of loss. This can lead to the strong emotional reactions seen in PBPD as a way of protecting themselves from further emotional pain. Additionally, if a child's needs are not regularly met, they can develop an inflated sense of privilege and an expectation of having their needs met quickly. This can add to the frustration and anger they experience when things don't go their way.

4. Self-Destructive BPD

Borderline Personality Disorder (BPD) can appear in various ways, and self-destructive BPD presents a unique set of difficulties. Individuals with this subtype struggle with a powerful mix of self-loathing, emotional instability, and a tendency for dangerous behaviors. This situation can leave them stuck in a loop of self-sabotage and mental turmoil. They often deal with a deep well of hatred and anger. These emotions can stem from past experiences of abuse or rejection, leaving them feeling deeply dangerous and unlovable. This can appear in a persistent sense of moodiness, a struggle to maintain a stable sense of self, and an intense fear of being abandoned by those they care about. The mental turmoil within can build like pressure in a cooker. Often, individuals with self-destructive BPD bottle up their feelings, expecting bad responses from others. However, this mental denial can only hold for so long. Eventually, the pressure becomes overwhelming and breaks into bouts of anger, self-harming behaviors, or rash decisions.

Paradoxically, some people with self-destructive BPD can experience times of high, almost manic energy. This can appear as happiness, a feeling of being unstoppable, or a desperate desire for excitement. However, these highs are often brief and can lead to even greater lows when the inevitable crash comes. This emotional rollercoaster can drive further risky behaviors like drug abuse, careless spending, or self-harm, in a confused attempt to control their feelings.

The roots of self-destructive BPD can often be linked back to experiences of trauma, neglect, or abuse in childhood. These tragedies can leave permanent scars on a person's sense of self-worth and ability to trust others. The world can feel fundamentally dangerous, and connections fragile. This can lead to a skewed view of good events. Because their past relationships were often wild and uncertain, they can struggle to think that good experiences can be safe or permanent. As a result, they can mentally destroy any progress they make, returning to old patterns of self-destruction as a way of unknowingly recreating the chaos they experienced in their youth.

Moving On

As we end this study of Borderline Personality Disorder (BPD), I want to leave you with a message of hope and support. We've covered a lot of ground, from knowing the core features of BPD to the varied ways it can appear in an individual's life. We've also addressed common myths and removed the shame regarding this illness. In the next part, we'll dig deeper into the possible reasons for BPD. Understanding the factors that might contribute to the growth of this condition can allow us to create even more effective treatment methods. Join me as we study the possible genetic, cultural, and neurological factors that might play a role in BPD.

Remember, a diagnosis of BPD is not a life sentence. It simply means you have a special set of tasks to manage. The good news is that you can learn to control your feelings, build healthy relationships, and live a satisfying life with the right help and care.

Here are some key lessons from this chapter:

• ***BPD is a complicated condition:*** There's no single "face" of BPD. It appears differently in each person, with a range of mental, behavioral, and social situations.

• ***You are not alone:*** BPD is a more common problem than you might think. Many people deal with BPD, and there are successful solutions available.

• ***Understanding is key:*** By understanding the different forms of BPD, we can move beyond labels and focus on building individual treatment plans.

• ***Treatment works:*** There is hope. With treatment, such as Dialectical Behavior treatment (DBT), you can develop useful skills for controlling your feelings, regulating your actions, and building good relationships.

If you think you or someone you know might be suffering from BPD, please reach out for professional help. Don't hesitate to seek help from a skilled therapist who can provide a thorough review and build a treatment plan tailored to your particular needs. You are not defined by your illness. BPD may be a part of you, but it doesn't have to define your future. With information, support, and the right treatment method, you can learn to handle BPD and live a life filled with meaning and connection.

CHAPTER 3

The Roots of BPD: Exploring Causes and Risk Factors

We looked at the many facets of borderline personality disorder (BPD) in the previous chapter. We observed that there are several ways in which the disorder might present itself, including a broad spectrum of emotional, behavioral, and relational experiences. I want to now turn our attention to comprehending the possible seeds that might be sowed and the elements that could lead to the development of BPD as we begin this next chapter.

Now here's the thing: BPD is not a straightforward illness with a single, obvious etiology. It resembles a multi-piece, intricate puzzle. We can learn a lot by investigating the risk variables and probable underlying causes. Consider it as gardening maintenance. If we limit our attention to the visible flowers (the manifestations), we can overlook important details on the conditions of the soil, exposure to sunshine, and watering requirements (the root causes).

Knowing these fundamental causes gives us two important advantages. First of all, it enables us to create more thorough treatment programs that cater to the unique requirements of every patient. Secondly, it cultivates comprehension and empathy. Understanding that a complex web of circumstances often contributes to borderline personality disorder (BPD) might help us get beyond judgment and foster a more healing environment.

Here, we'll look at a few of the factors that are relevant, such as neurobiological elements, environmental effects, and genetics. It's important to keep in mind that although these variables can not directly cause BPD, they can raise the likelihood of the disorder or influence how it presents itself. Remember that every person's experience is different and maintain an open mind while you investigate these possible foundations. Finding fault or easy solutions is not our aim; instead, we want to learn more about BPD and the people who deal with its difficulties.

Exploring Causes and Risk Factors

Many techniques have been used to investigate the genesis and causes of Borderline Personality Disorder (BPD). Different methods have been used by researchers to try to figure out why certain people have this condition. Family studies have been one significant line of inquiry. These investigations have repeatedly shown that a large number of people with BPD have substantial difficulties or disturbances throughout their formative years. These disturbances can include traumatizing events, erratic caring, or unstable familial situations. This shows that a major contributing factor to the development of BPD can be the environment. Although research indicates a complex interaction of biological, genetic, and environmental variables, the precise causes of BPD are yet unknown

BIOLOGICAL ROOTS

Have you ever thought about why some families seem to have quite different personalities? A lot of people think about that question, and your grandmother was partly right when she said that. Even though the things we do in life do shape us, a new study shows that our genes (biology) and our surroundings also play a big role in how we grow, including our risk of Borderline Personality Disorder (BPD).

This is how to think about it: Think of your personality as a lovely garden. The genes you get from your parents give you a base, but how well your garden grows depends a lot on how well you take care of it (environment). When we look at biological risk factors for BPD, there are two main ones:

1. Genetic or inherited factors:

Just like the color of your eyes or the pattern of your hair, some of your personality tendencies are affected by the genes you receive from your parents. A recent study shows a major genetic tendency to BPD, meaning there's a higher chance of getting it if a close cousin has the disease. But what role do genes play? Imagine your genes as a complicated set of rules that guide the growth and function of your brain. These directions determine how your brain cells (neurons) interact with each other, regulate different chemicals (neurotransmitters), and eventually affect how you think, feel, and behave.

Scientists think that differences in certain genes that affect these brain processes can be linked to BPD. Here are some key areas of research:

• ***Emotion Regulation:*** Certain gene differences might affect how your brain processes and manages feelings. This could lead to a heightened emotional reaction, trouble calming down from strong feelings, or problems safely sharing emotions.

• ***Impulse Control:*** Some genes might affect the brain's ability to control emotions and make reasonable choices. This could appear as rash behaviors, trouble handling anger, or participating in risky activities.

• ***Relationship Building:*** Genes might also play a part in how we form and keep good relationships. Variations in certain genes could add to problems with trust, fear of loss, or strong, shaky relationships.

It's important to understand that these are just possible effects, not promises. This is how to think about it: Imagine receiving a gene that makes you more susceptible to cold weather (greater risk). If you live in a warm area (protected setting), you might never feel the effects of that gene. Similarly, having a genetic tendency to BPD doesn't mean you'll develop the condition.

Here's the key: Environment plays a key role in how these genetic weaknesses appear. If someone with a genetic predisposition suffers a difficult or painful childhood, for example, it can increase the risk of BPD forming.

The good news? By knowing these genetic effects, we can create more focused treatment methods. For example, treatment can help people learn good coping strategies for controlling feelings, regulating urges, and building better relationships, even if they have a genetic tendency to BPD. Remember, BPD is not simply a matter of genes. It's a complex relationship between genes and the surroundings. By recognizing the role of genetics, we can build a more complete knowledge of the condition and enable people to take control of their mental health.

2. Abnormal Brain Development:

While the exact causes of BPD are still being studied, a new study shows that sometimes, problems can appear during pregnancy that affect the growing brain of the baby. These problems can raise the risk of BPD, but it's important to understand that they're not the main reason and don't ensure someone will develop the condition.

Here's a closer look at how abnormal brain growth might play a role:

Disruptions in Neural Pathways: The human brain is a complex network of linked paths that allow information to flow between different areas. These pathways are important for controlling feelings, managing urges, and building good partnerships. Studies show that BPD might be linked to changes in these brain processes, which could be caused by different factors during pregnancy. Imagine your brain is like a big city with different neighborhoods responsible for different things. These neighborhoods are linked by roads that allow texts to move back and forth. In a healthy brain, these "highways" (neural paths) are smooth and efficient, letting information move smoothly.

Now, a BPD study shows that sometimes, problems during pregnancy might disrupt these routes. Think of it like cracks or road closures. The information (emotions, urges, social cues) can get stuck or take longer to get where they need to go. This might explain why some people with BPD fight to handle their feelings or control their urges. The words telling them to calm down or think before they act might not be getting through as fast. Similarly, issues building good relationships could be linked to problems with the "highways" that help us understand and connect with others.

It's important to understand that these are just possible delays, not full roadblocks. The brain is pretty amazing and can often find ways to move messages, even if the main roads have some problems. This is why the surroundings plays such a big part. A helpful and caring setting can be like building new roads or fixing potholes, helping the brain create better ways to control feelings, urges, and relationships.

Neurotransmitter Imbalances: Our brains rely on a careful mix of chemicals called neurotransmitters to work properly. These chemicals act as messengers, sending information between brain cells. Some study shows that BPD might be linked to changes in certain chemicals, like serotonin or dopamine. These changes could lead to difficulty managing emotions, feeling reckless, or having trouble forming stable partnerships. Imagine your brain is like a big party with lots of different people (brain cells) talking to each other. To connect, they use special messengers called neurotransmitters. These messengers are like tiny boxes holding information about feelings, desires, and how to connect with others.

In a healthy brain, there's a good mix of these messages. However, some study shows that people with BPD might have problems with certain messengers, like serotonin or dopamine. Think of it like some envelopes getting lost or given too many times. This might explain why some people with BPD deal with their feelings. Canbe the "calm down" messages aren't getting delivered properly, making it harder to control their thoughts. Similarly, problems with impulse control could be like the "think before you act" texts not coming on time. Difficulties with relationships might be linked to issues with the messages that help us understand and connect with others.

These are just possible inequalities, not like a total shutdown of the party. The brain is pretty flexible and can sometimes find ways to use different messengers or shift messages even if there's a bit of a backlog. This is why the surroundings play a big part. A helpful setting can be like having extra agents on hand or improving the communication system, helping the brain create better ways to handle feelings, urges, and relationships.

Prenatal worry Exposure: If a pregnant person feels major worry during pregnancy, it can affect the growing baby' brain. This stress exposure might lead to changes in brain structure or chemical development, which could increase the chance of BPD later in life. It's important to note that not all stress during pregnancy results in these problems, and individual resolve plays a role. Imagine a baby growing inside a mommy's tummy. It's a cozy, safe place where the baby's brain is growing fast, learning everything it needs to know. But sometimes, if the mommy feels a lot of worry during pregnancy, it can be like a bumpy car ride for the baby's brain growth. This stress might not always cause problems, but some study shows it could affect how the baby's brain gets built or how it uses special chemicals called neurotransmitters (remember, those are like messages in the brain). These changes could raise the risk of BPD later in life.

Here's the important part: not all stress during pregnancy is dangerous. Think of it like this: some bumps on the road are just small and the baby's brain is pretty good at handling them. Plus, everyone is different – some kids (and their brains) are naturally more immune to stress than others. The key thing is to take care of the mom during pregnancy. By controlling stress and providing a calm, loving setting, we can give the baby the best chance for healthy brain growth. And even if there were some bumps along the way, remember, the brain is amazing and can still learn and grow with the right help.

Now, let's face the big question: Does this mean that if you had a tough birth or were exposed to fetal stress, you're sure to develop BPD? Absolutely not!

Here's why:

• ***The Brain is Remarkably Plastic:*** The human brain has an amazing ability to shift and change, especially during early growth. This means that even if there were some problems during pregnancy, the brain can still build good coping strategies over time.

• ***Environment Plays a Big Role:*** Just like with genetic factors, the environment works with possible risks caused by abnormal brain development. A helpful and caring environment can create a cushion against these weaknesses, while a stressed or painful childhood can increase the risk of BPD forming.

By knowing the possible role of abnormal brain development in BPD, we can:

• ***Promote Early Intervention:*** If a child has a history of prenatal problems, early assistance, and support programs can help promote healthy brain development and build resilience.

• ***Develop More Comprehensive Treatment Plans:*** Understanding the basic brain processes of BPD can help us tailor treatment methods to address specific problems, such as emotional management or impulse control.

• ***Reduce Stigma:*** Knowing that BPD might have a biological component can help us move away from the idea that it's a personal failure and instead view it as a complex disease affected by various factors.

While there are complex chemical factors at play in BPD, it's important to understand that they're just one piece of the picture. The relationship between these biological weaknesses and external factors eventually forms an individual's risk of having the disease. The good news is that with ongoing study and a complete knowledge of BPD, we can create better treatment choices and enable people to lead fulfilling and healthy lives. While these biological factors can play a role, it's important to understand that BPD doesn't grow in a vacuum. Most experts think genetic causes hold more weight, but they don't act alone. Imagine those gene differences as weaknesses, like tiny plants. If a stressed setting – a harsh childhood experience, for example – acts like harsh weather, it can greatly impact how those weaknesses grow. For some people, these mixed factors can increase the chance of having BPD.

BPD often groups in families, meaning there's a higher chance of getting it if a close relative has it or a linked condition like bipolar disorder, drug abuse, or certain personality disorders. This shows a possible connection between the genes and brain processes involved in these diseases. Understanding these biological risk factors isn't about putting blame or making predictions. It's about getting useful ideas.

ENVIRONMENTAL ROOTS

We have discussed the possible impact that genes play in BPD, but the reality is that biology is not the only factor at play. Our life experiences, particularly those of our early years, can also have a big influence on our likelihood of getting the illness. Now let's look at a few environmental risk factors associated with BPD:

1. Early Loss or Separation:

A common occurrence in the lives of individuals with borderline personality disorder (BPD) is the early separation from one or both of their parents. Divorce, a parent's death, or even a circumstance in which a parent is physically present but emotionally unavailable can all result in this separation. Parents in these households either divorce or split or one parent passes away or leaves the family early on. Genetically transmitted mental problems, such as bipolar disorder, severe depression, alcoholism, or antisocial behaviors like crime, are present in some parents of patients with borderline disorder. Consider it akin to constructing a home. A durable construction needs a strong base. A child's foundation is made up of their parents' love, security, and unwavering care. However, it's like constructing a home on an unsteady foundation when a parent is missing, whether physically or emotionally.

This early separation can be associated with a higher risk of BPD for two key reasons:

Problems Developing a Robust Self-Concept: childs who experience early separation can find it difficult to develop a strong sense of identity and self-worth. What if a young toddler asked themselves, "Who am I?" It might be challenging to respond to that question if they haven't had constant affection and support to build a foundation.

Problems with Trust: It might be challenging for a child to learn to trust others when the ones they most depend on aren't always there for them. Imagine being afraid and alone because the people you thought would be protecting you turned out to be untrustworthy. A child can find it difficult to establish trustworthy and healthy connections as a result of this in the future. It's crucial to keep in mind that early loss or separation does not always result in BPD. But it can also be a danger factor, particularly if the child doesn't have other supporting family members, aunts, uncles, or close friends in their lives. The good news is that people with BPD can learn to forge better connections and a stronger sense of self with the help of treatment and the appropriate support network.

2. Childhood Abuse:

Sadly, a large number of individuals with BPD have been the victims of abuse at some point in their lives. This might take the form of physical abuse (being struck or injured), mental abuse (often being screamed at or put down), or even sexual abuse. While long-term physical abuse is more likely in males with the illness, repeated sexual abuse is more common in women. A family member or someone from outside the family can abuse someone in this way. Long-term sexual abuse, particularly incest, is linked to a higher risk of self-harm and suicide in individuals diagnosed with borderline personality disorder.

Imagine a child who lives in their own house, a place where they should feel secure, but instead, they find it frightening and unreliable. Abuse destroys a child's sense of security and faith in the outside world. A kid cannot flourish in an abusive atmosphere, just as a flower cannot flourish in a severe storm.

Abuse can have the following effects on a person with BPD:

• ***Constantly feeling tense:*** Imagine being unable to predict when a negative event can occur. Being vigilant all the time might make it difficult to unwind and feel secure.

• ***Having trouble feeling loved:*** The experience of abuse can rob a kid of their right to feel loved or that anybody cares for them.

• ***Hard-to-control strong emotions:*** Victims of abuse can sometimes feel difficult-to-control feelings like fear, despair, or fury. They can find it challenging to know how to handle these emotions healthily.

• ***Relationship issues:*** It might be difficult for someone to trust others if they can't trust those who were meant to look out for them. This might make it challenging to establish wholesome connections.

The favorable tidings? Although being abused as a kid is a horrible event, it does not guarantee that a person will always have BPD. Individuals who have experienced abuse can develop better connections, feel safer in the world, and acquire good coping techniques via therapy.

3. Ineffective Parenting:

It's no secret that effective parenting is essential! Regrettably, some BPD patients have had inconsistent or unsupportive parents in the past. Many BPD sufferers did not have the kind of upbringing that supports their development into robust, healthy adults. It's possible that their parents weren't particularly receptive, which means they weren't truly aware of their wants or emotions. Or maybe they were unloving, which would have made it difficult for the child to feel comfortable and protected. Some parents can find it challenging to be effective role models because they are dealing with personal issues. childrens need consistency and limits to flourish. It might be challenging for kids to pick up good coping strategies for handling relationships and emotions when these are absent. Consider it similar to learning how to ride a bike. Someone who can guide you, support you and acknowledge your accomplishments is what you need. It can be challenging for a kid to develop positive relationships and acquire appropriate coping mechanisms when parents are unable to provide for them.

When children don't get the proper parenting, the following things can happen:

• *Difficulty controlling emotions:* It might be difficult to know how to handle strong emotions like anger, grief, or frustration if you don't learn effective coping mechanisms.

• *Imprecise boundaries:* Consider engaging in a game with no set rules. Yes, it's perplexing. Parents must set clear limits for their children for them to know what is and is not acceptable. It might be challenging to negotiate relationships later in life without them.

• *Feeling lost or alone:* Children who don't get assistance from their parents can come to believe that they are alone. This might be a frightening and lonesome sensation.

The key point to keep in mind is that growing and healing are possible for those who did not have the finest upbringing. People with BPD can develop solid relationships, acquire appropriate coping techniques, and feel better about themselves with the help of treatment and support. There is no vacuum in which these environmental influences exist. They interact with each other in a similar way to genetics. A child who is genetically predisposed to BPD can be more susceptible to the harmful consequences of having a rough upbringing.

4. Pressures from Society:

Alright, so we've discussed how certain events throughout infancy might raise the likelihood of developing BPD. But there's more to think about BPD sufferers can experience more stress as a result of modern society. Moreover, conventional networks of support such as close-knit communities or extended families can not exist as much as they once did. This implies that individuals can not have the same opportunities for good impacts and safety nets that previous generations had.

Therapist Theodore Millon identified a few aspects of contemporary culture that might make matters more difficult:

• *Constant Change:* With new technology, evolving morals, and fluctuating expectations, it seems like everything in our world is changing all the time. Imagine that everything around you is constantly shifting when you already feel like you're on unstable footing! For anybody, particularly someone with BPD who can already battle with a sense of self, this can be very perplexing and stressful.

• *Fewer Safety Nets:* It's possible that in the past, close-knit communities or extended families provided greater assistance to individuals. Families these days are often dispersed, and communities can not be as close-knit. This implies that there can be fewer "safety nets" for developing kids in need of supportive adults. Consider it like walking a tightrope. It might be more frightening if you're already unsteady on your feet and there are fewer people around to catch you if you fall.

Despite the stress of contemporary life, there are still strategies to establish a solid support network. Through therapy, persons with BPD might learn effective coping mechanisms. They can also locate support networks or form close connections with like-minded individuals. Recall that you can succeed in today's environment with the correct support and that BPD does not define you.

The good news is this:

Even if they have an effect, these contextual variables can not always indicate BPD. Some individuals have extraordinary resilience and, with the correct assistance, can get through very trying times. By comprehending these elements, we can create more effective treatment strategies. Through therapy, people with BPD can acquire good coping mechanisms for their emotions, strengthen their relationships with others, and deal with trauma from the past.

It's important to keep in mind that BPD is a complicated disorder with a variety of underlying causes. By recognizing the influence of both genetics and the environment, we can develop a more comprehensive knowledge of BPD and enable people to recover and flourish.

BPD AND THE BRAIN: WHEN EXPERIENCES DISRUPT NEURAL CONNECTIONS

We've discussed the connection between DNA and BPD, but events throughout your life have a big impact too. Let's explore how these events alter your brain and how BPD can be related to this.

The Brain: An Interconnected System

The human brain is an amazing example of intricacy, with connections between various areas constantly growing and changing. Neural pathways are these connections between different parts of the brain that function as information highways, coordinating our ideas, feelings, and actions. The stronger the connected pathways develop, the more we utilize a certain ability or go through a given event. knowledge of how our life experiences might affect the brain and perhaps contribute to the development of BPD requires a knowledge of the "use it or lose it" concept.

Consider the brain as an enormous, intricately linked network of neurons, akin to a busy city. Within this city, various districts correspond to different brain areas that are in charge of tasks like memory, emotion control, and sensory processing. Information can move easily between these areas thanks to neural connections acting as the roads. For example, learning a new language causes certain brain areas that are involved in understanding, pronunciation, and memory retrieval to become stronger. These pathways become more effective with further practice, making it easier for us to speak and comprehend the language.

Positive experiences help to fortify brain connections, while long-term negative experiences—like those often described by people with borderline personality disorder (BPD)—can be harmful. Consider these unpleasant encounters as roadblocks or hiccups on the information superhighways. For instance, evidence points to the possibility that people with BPD who were traumatized as children can have less effective or weaker neural circuits in the areas of the brain linked to emotional regulation. This can help to explain why some people with BPD find it difficult to control strong emotions like grief or rage.

Neural pathways are a notion that goes beyond language acquisition. Consider picking up a new instrument for music. The connections connecting the brain areas in charge of your motor abilities, vision, and auditory processing are initially poor. These pathways become stronger with experience, which improves your coordination and accuracy when playing. This demonstrates the brain's amazing plasticity—its capacity to adjust and change throughout life. Therapists can create focused therapies to enhance certain neural pathways and foster resilience in people with borderline personality disorder (BPD) by knowing how events change our brain networks.

The Significance of Our Past Experiences

Knowing how life events affect the brain is essential for psychotherapists, particularly when dealing with clients who have borderline personality disorder (BPD). A network of neural pathways powers our brains, and these pathways are continually shaped by the experiences we have throughout our lives, much like fragile seedlings in a garden.

Good Feelings: Nourishing Brain Circuits for Emotional Health

These brain circuits depend on feeling supported, reaching objectives, and having a sense of community as essential nutrients. Envision a solid, encouraging family setting. This creates favorable experiences that strengthen neural connections in areas of the brain linked to emotional control and self-worth. It's similar to planting our emotional well-being seedlings in healthy soil with plenty of sunlight. It is critical to comprehend this relationship in BPD since emotional dysregulation is a central symptom. One of the main challenges for many people with BPD is managing powerful emotions; stronger emotional regulation pathways can help with this. • Negative Experiences: The Thorns and Storms that Disrupt Development

Regretfully, not every person lives in a supportive environment. In our mental garden, persistent stress, abuse, neglect, and other unfavorable events are similar to severe storms or prickly weeds. These encounters have the potential to harm growing brain circuits and impair normal function. According to research, early trauma can have interfered with the development of neural connections in brain areas linked to emotion regulation and fear response in certain people with BPD. Consider a storm-beaten seedling that is having difficulty developing into a robust plant. This disturbance can be the cause of some BPD patients' inability to control strong emotions or increased fear in certain circumstances.

The Influence of Neuroplasticity: Fostering Adaptability in the Face of Adversity

The good news is that the brain's amazing capacity for adaptation and change persists throughout adulthood. We refer to this as neuroplasticity. It's similar to taking care of an overgrown garden—even after a storm. We can reinforce current routes and foster new development with the correct care and assistance. In cases of BPD in particular, early intervention is essential since it enables us to treat any possible harm and encourage normal brain development.

We can create BPD treatment programs that are more successful by comprehending how events alter our brain structure. Individuals with BPD can learn how: in therapy

• *Control Your Emotions:* Learn effective coping strategies to handle strong feelings like fear, grief, or rage.

• *Practice mindfulness:* Become more conscious of your thoughts, emotions, and physical sensations right now.

• *Communicate Effectively:* Develop aggressive communication techniques to accurately communicate your demands and limits.

• *Create Robust Relationships:* Establish more intimate and trustworthy ways of interacting with others.

• *Increase Self-Esteem:* Develop a more robust feeling of identity and self-worth.

Comorbid Conditions: Dissociative Identity Disorder and Others

We've discussed the main signs and possible causes of BPD, or borderline personality disorder. However, BPD is seldom isolated. Many people with BPD also have other mental health diagnoses, a situation known as comorbid disorders. It is essential to comprehend these co-occurring disorders for both efficient therapy and general health.

Disorder of Dissociative Identity (DID)

The existence of two or more separate identities or personality states that have the ability to take control of a person's actions, thoughts, and emotions is what defines DID, formerly known as Multiple Personality Disorder. In addition to memory lapses and a feeling of being detached from reality, people with DID often suffer a disturbance in their sense of self and identity.

The Link Between DID and BPD: A Complex Relationship

Certain traits, such as emotional turbulence, impulsive behavior, and unstable relationships, are shared by both BPD and DID. The main distinction, however, is that DID involves separate identities. Even though various symptoms could coexist, it's crucial to realize that they each reflect a distinct underlying process.

• *Trauma: A Possible Cause of Both Illnesses*

Even though the etiology of DID and BPD are complicated, research indicates that trauma, especially throughout infancy, could have a major role. People who have BPD often talk about being emotionally abused, neglected, or invalidated. These events can significantly affect a growing brain, perhaps affecting how relationships are established, emotions are controlled, and self-identity is developed.

• *Using dissociation as a coping strategy*

When faced with severe trauma, dissociation can occur as a coping strategy. A disconnection from one's ideas, emotions, memories, or sense of self is referred to as dissociation. It can be a means of getting away from upsetting situations or intense feelings. In DID, recurring dissociation can sometimes result in the emergence of unique identities as a means for the person to compartmentalize intense feelings and experiences.

How BPD Symptoms Can Be Associated with DID

For those with BPD, the difficulties might be exacerbated by the existence of DID. How to do it is as follows:

• *Emotional Fragmentation:* People with DID can have distinct emotional experiences, which can exacerbate emotional instability and make it harder to control strong emotions.

• *Identity Confusion:* BPD core symptoms such as feelings of emptiness and instability can be exacerbated by the fractured sense of self associated with DID.

• *Compulsive Behaviors:* Certain DID personalities can exhibit impulsive behavior more often, which exacerbates the self-control issues common in BPD.

• *Dissociation as an Escape:* In both DID and BPD, dissociation can develop as a default coping strategy for intense emotions, impeding normal emotional processing and resulting in further emotional dysregulation.

Treatment Ideas: Using a Holistic Perspective

Treatment for DID and BPD that is both thorough and empathetic is necessary. Therapy can address the difficulties of these co-occurring illnesses in the following ways:

Trauma-focused therapy: Healing requires an examination and processing of prior trauma. People who are seeking assistance in comprehending how their prior experiences can be influencing their current feelings and actions might benefit from therapies such as Trauma-Focused Cognitive Behavioral Therapy (TF-CBT).

Dialectical Behavior Therapy (DBT): DBT gives people the tools they need to better communicate, control their emotions, endure discomfort, and form wholesome relationships. These are necessary abilities for DID as well as BPD.

Integration Work (DID): A therapist can collaborate with a patient in DID therapy to facilitate communication between the many identities and eventually help them merge into a more unified sense of self.

Creating a Supporting Network: Keeping stable relationships can be difficult for those with both BPD and DID. Through therapy, people can learn constructive coping strategies and how to communicate with others to create helpful relationships.

Extremely Common Comorbidities: A complex web of difficulties

Nonetheless, BPD patients often have more comorbid diagnoses than those with other mental health disorders do on average. A deeper look at a few of the most common comorbidities is provided below:

Post-Traumatic Stress Disorder (PTSD)

A significant proportion of individuals with Borderline Personality Disorder (BPD) have experienced childhood trauma, abuse, or neglect. Both PTSD and BPD can develop as a result of these situations. Emotional dysregulation and dissociation that can occur in BPD patients can be made more difficult by PTSD symptoms such as nightmares, flashbacks, and hypervigilance. Particularly for those who haven't had any training in mental health, post-traumatic stress disorder (PTSD) and borderline personality disorder (BPD) can sometimes seem identical. Intense emotions, trouble controlling emotions, and problematic relationships can all be present in both. It is vital to comprehend the main differences between them.

How each condition's sufferers react after their trauma has healed is one important distinction. When a traumatic event is well processed, it can greatly lessen the severity and recurrence of emotional flashbacks and triggers in a person with PTSD. They start to feel more in control of how they respond to the past. On the other hand, even once trauma has been treated, people with BPD can find it difficult to completely stop feeling bad. They often react emotionally in more general ways that are less dependent on particular stimuli. To control their emotions in the here and now, they place a strong emphasis on creating good coping strategies.

Though the underlying reasons and experiences are different, mood swings can occur in both BPD and PTSD. Mood fluctuations in people with PTSD often happen in reaction to being reminded of their traumatic experiences. When provoked, they can feel a quick flood of dread, wrath, or worry. However, they can usually bring their emotional state back to normal using self-soothing methods and grounding exercises. Mood fluctuations in BPD sufferers are more closely associated with their general emotional susceptibility than with particular triggers. Based on imagined threats, abandonment anxieties, or interpersonal slights, they could go through dramatic emotional changes. Long-term treatment and skill development are necessary for managing these strong emotions.

Relationship problems can arise from erratic emotional reactions in both PTSD and BPD. Fear of coming into contact with triggers can cause social disengagement or avoidance in those with PTSD. Some can not comprehend the reason behind the emotional outbursts. Family members can feel as if the person with BPD is treading carefully because of their severe outbursts of rage, possessiveness, and desire for control. The causes of these actions vary, however. When it comes to particular risks associated with their trauma, people with PTSD are responding, but those with BPD are probably reacting out of fear of being abandoned or a desperate desire to feel protected.

Major Depressive Disorder (MDD)

There is a possibility that borderline personality disorder (BPD) and major depressive disorder (MDD) can sometimes coexist. According to studies, 38% to 71% of persons who have one of these disorders also have the other. Long-term episodes of depression, which are defined as two weeks or more, are characterized by feelings of melancholy, boredom, exhaustion, and difficulty sleeping. It is a severe kind of depression that can affect a person's everyday life, as implied by the name. For an appropriate diagnosis and successful treatment, it is essential to comprehend how they overlap and vary from one another.

The symptoms of BPD and MDD might be similar, including exhaustion, poor mood, and sleep issues. It can be difficult to distinguish between the two situations because of this overlap. But a deeper examination shows some important differences. A person with MDD has widespread, chronic depression that lasts for at least two weeks at a time. Although it has a major effect on a person's day-to-day activities, the emotional state is usually steady throughout this time. On the other hand, there is a much greater level of emotional instability in those who have BPD. They can experience abrupt and extreme mood fluctuations, sometimes in a single day. This emotional dysregulation is a defining characteristic of BPD and a crucial way it differs from MDD.

A major source of emotional distress for those with BPD is a deep-seated dread of being abandoned. A habit of passionate and unstable relationships is fueled by this dread. People often do this because they fear being rejected, which can lead them to idealize someone one minute and despise them the next. Aggressive acts, impulsive behaviors, and violent outbursts can result from this. Following the incident, they experience intense regret and guilt, which feeds into their fear of being abandoned and starts a vicious cycle that they can soon have to break. Although depression is a common symptom of MDD, it is not as intensely reactive to emotions as BPD. A persistent sensation of melancholy, despair, and a lack of interest in once-enjoyable activities can be used to characterize the poor mood associated with MDD. This particular characteristic of MDD's low mood aids in setting it apart from BPD sufferers' emotional instability.

The co-occurrence of BPD and MDD creates particular therapeutic difficulties. But there's still hope. An expert in mental health can carry out a comprehensive assessment to establish the best diagnosis and create a customized treatment strategy. Therapy techniques like cognitive behavioral therapy (CBT), which assists people in recognizing and challenging unfavorable thinking patterns that affect their mood, can be beneficial for both illnesses. To assist control of neurotransmitters and lessen depressive symptoms, other therapy methods for MDD, such as medication management, can be taken into consideration.

Dialectical behavior therapy, or DBT, is a very successful treatment method for BPD. DBT gives people skills in interpersonal communication, distress tolerance, emotional regulation, and mindfulness. With these abilities, they can better control their strong emotions, strengthen their bonds with others, and end the vicious cycle of self-destructive behavior. It can be especially difficult when BPD and MDD co-occur. Both disorders are complicated. However, people can significantly improve their mood, emotional regulation, and interpersonal dynamics with a thorough grasp of these problems and a dedication to evidence-based therapy. Please get in touch with a mental health professional if you or someone you know is experiencing signs of BPD, MDD, or both. There is support available, and you are not alone.

Bipolar Disorder

At first look, bipolar disorder and borderline personality disorder (BPD) can seem to be comparable. Mood swings and emotional dysregulation are features of both diseases. There are some significant differences between the two, however.

Rapid and drastic mood swings are common in people with BPD, sometimes occurring in a single day or even an hour. They might go from extreme melancholy to unexpected joy and back again. Their conduct is greatly impacted by these emotional swings. For example, they can spend impulsively to cope during a melancholy episode, and then feel guilty and regretful when their mood swings. This sets off a never-ending spiral of emotional upheaval. On the other hand, bipolar disorder is distinguished by discrete, protracted episodes of mania or depression. Bipolar disorder is characterized by manic episodes, which can extend for days or even weeks at a time. In addition to dangerous or impulsive activities like excessive spending, gambling, or sexual promiscuity, people can have extreme energy, racing thoughts, and hurried speech during these episodes. Their relationships, finances, and general well-being can all suffer significantly as a result of these behaviors. But manic episodes in bipolar disorder are longer-lasting than the transient mood swings of borderline personality disorder (BPD), and they can also be accompanied by sleep difficulties, racing thoughts, and a grandiose sense of self.

The difficulties in distinguishing between bipolar disorder and borderline personality disorder (BPD) were shown via a case study. Jane, a 22-year-old college student, presented in the case with a history of severe emotional swings. Jane might experience dramatic mood swings in a matter of hours, from euphoria and grandiosity to deep misery and self-deprecation. Her moods were so erratic that it left her feeling lost and powerless. She also had patterns of unstable interpersonal interactions, idealizing new friends and then abruptly shifting to great anger and resentment, which resulted in numerous disputes and damaged relationships.

Impulsive actions were another way that Jane's emotional instability showed themselves. In a mistaken effort to ease her emotional suffering, she can resort to impulsive behaviors like excessive spending or drug abuse, or she can withdraw from social interactions during depressed periods. These actions were always accompanied by intense emotions of humiliation and remorse. Seeking to address these difficulties, Jane presented to a mental health expert. However, the first examination resulted in a misdiagnosis of bipolar illness based on her high emotional reactions and fast mood swings. Consequently, Jane was administered medication commonly used for bipolar illness, which proved unsuccessful and created unpleasant side effects.

Dissatisfied with the lack of progress and the possibility of pharmaceutical side effects, Jane sought a second opinion from a mental health specialist specializing in personality disorders. This new doctor undertook a more extensive examination, looking not just into Jane's emotional experiences but also her interpersonal patterns and behavioral inclinations. After a thorough assessment, BPD was diagnosed. Jane was able to start evidence-based therapy designed especially for BPD after receiving an appropriate diagnosis. Jane had dialectical behavior therapy (DBT) to help her learn how to better communicate, control her emotional dysregulation, and create healthy coping strategies. Jane gained the ability to recognize her emotional triggers, create practical plans for controlling her feelings, and create more enduring and satisfying relationships thanks to DBT.

The example of Jane highlights the need for a thorough assessment by licensed mental health providers to distinguish BPD from bipolar illness. Although strong emotions and mood swings can be symptoms of either disorder, there are substantial differences in the underlying causes and treatment modalities. A precise diagnosis establishes the best course of action for therapy, which can greatly enhance a person's capacity to control their symptoms and create a more satisfying existence.

Although bipolar illness and borderline personality disorder pose difficulties, there are viable therapy alternatives. Dialectical behavior therapy, or DBT, is a very successful treatment for BPD. DBT gives people skills in interpersonal communication, distress tolerance, emotional regulation, and mindfulness. These abilities enable people to control their strong emotions, create wholesome connections, and stop engaging in self-destructive activities. Often, treating bipolar illness involves both psychotherapy and pharmaceutical management. Antipsychotics and mood stabilizers can help control mood fluctuations and stop manic or depressed episodes. Furthermore, therapeutic modalities such as cognitive behavioral therapy (CBT) might assist patients in recognizing and addressing the negative thinking patterns that underlie their mood swings. Accurate diagnosis and successful treatment depend on an understanding of the differences between bipolar illness and borderline personality disorder. Even though emotional dysregulation is a feature of both illnesses, mood swings' characteristics and lengths vary greatly. Mental health practitioners can guarantee that people get the best care and support for their unique needs by acknowledging these variations.

Substance Use Disorders

Drug addiction, also referred to as substance use disorder (SUD), is an intricate medical condition marked by an impaired capacity to regulate the use of drugs, whether legal or illicit, notwithstanding the possibility of damage. This is a subject that is widely discussed in our culture, from academic studies to popular media depictions in films, TV series, music videos, and documentaries. Many people who suffer from borderline personality disorder (BPD) also have drug use disorders. Substance abuse is frequently attractive to people with BPD because they want to dull their emotional suffering and self-medicate. Because of this overlap, BPD can be misdiagnosed as SUD alone. According to statistics, 14% to 72% of individuals with BPD also struggle with a co-occurring drug use disorder. The exact prevalence might change based on co-morbid illnesses and other susceptible factors.

This co-occurrence is mostly attributed to impulsivity which is a defining characteristic of BPD. Drugs are often seen as an easy and fast way to control emotions, even if the effects are just momentary. But there's an important difference to be made when diagnosing BPD. According to the BPD diagnostic criteria, impulsivity must appear in at least one domain outside of drug use. This impulsivity might show itself, for instance, in careless spending, unsafe sexual activity, binge eating, or unsafe driving. Impulsive desires are widespread and don't only pertain to one action in BPD. In an effort to manage intense feelings, a person with BPD can go on a shopping spree or overindulge in food, rather than only abusing drugs. Rather than just drug abuse, the existence of these more generalized impulsive behaviors would suggest a BPD diagnosis.

An in-depth examination of the elements causing this co-occurrence is provided below:

• *Emotional dysregulation:* People with BPD find it difficult to control their strong feelings. Substance usage can be strongly encouraged as it provides a momentary reprieve from these intense emotions.

• *Impulsivity:* Despite the possible drawbacks, people with BPD are more likely to take substances in an attempt to get instant satisfaction due to their impulsive nature.

• ***Misguided Efforts at Self-Soothing:*** Misuse of substances to self-soothe and ease emotional pain can go wrong. But this often results in a more severe emotional dysregulation and dependency cycle.

• ***Difficulties in interactions:*** BPD is often accompanied by turbulent interpersonal interactions, which can exacerbate feelings of loneliness and isolation and increase the need to use drugs as a kind of self-medication.

The Value of Precise Diagnosis

Getting a proper diagnosis is essential to creating a successful treatment strategy. If BPD is mistakenly identified as a drug use disorder alone, emotional dysregulation and impulsivity will remain untreated. Appropriate treatment techniques can be determined by a mental health expert doing a thorough examination that distinguishes between the two illnesses.

Anxiety Disorders

Anxiety is a common human emotion that is defined by uncertainty, worry, and nervousness. But for those who suffer from anxiety disorders, these emotions intensify, becoming much more noticeable, and last longer. Anxiety disorders are characterized by excessive, uncontrolled dread that interferes with ordinary functioning, in contrast to the transient concerns of normal living. Over time, these fears can even become more severe, severely affecting a person's capacity to manage their relationships, jobs, and general well-being.

Anxiety disorders come in several forms, each with unique traits of its own. Panic disorder, social anxiety disorder (SAD), phobias, and generalized anxiety disorder (GAD) are a few prevalent kinds. These disorders can present in many different ways, but they are all characterized by excessive and ongoing anxiety and concern, as well as physical symptoms such as tightness in the muscles, a fast heartbeat, and shortness of breath. The acute feelings of terror and emotions that people with BPD experience can first resemble the worries linked to anxiety disorders. Feelings of concern, dread, and helplessness are common to both diseases. For example, if a person with BPD fears being abandoned by a loved one, they can suffer severe anxiety. They can also experience debilitating guilt after an impulsive outburst. Additionally, they could find it difficult to control their emotions and behave healthily.

Given these similar characteristics, it seems sense that BPD is sometimes misdiagnosed as an anxiety condition. Still, there is an important difference in how long and how widespread these apprehensive sensations last.

The Main Distinguisher: How long does anxiety last?

The length of time that anxiety symptoms persist is what distinguishes anxiety disorders from BPD. The anxious mood is noticeably more common and persistent in those with anxiety disorders. The majority of anxiety disorders have diagnostic criteria that need symptoms to be significantly present for at least six months. On the other hand, people with BPD often experience acute feelings and anxiety that are more sporadic and fleeting. Even while these emotional storms can be quite disruptive, they usually pass quickly.

Above and Beyond the Common: Investigating Less Common Comorbidities

I spoke about a few of the most prevalent illnesses that can coexist with BPD. However, the field of comorbidity is broad. Other conditions that can sometimes co-occur with BPD include the following:

Eating Disorder

Borderline personality disorder (BPD) and eating disorders are two different mental health diseases. They can, nonetheless, sometimes exhibit overlapping symptoms, which might result in a false positive. Comprehending the fundamental characteristics of any ailment is crucial for precise diagnosis and effective therapy. Severe disruptions in eating patterns, together with related thoughts and feelings, are the hallmarks of eating disorders, which are complex mental health illnesses. They are classified as severe and often deadly disorders by the National Institute of Mental Health (NIMH).

Typical eating problems consist of:

• *Anorexia Nervosa:* This disorder is characterized by a severe fear of gaining weight, which causes self-starvation and the maintenance of an unhealthy weight.

• *Bulimia Nervosa:* Consists of a cycle of binge eating and purging actions such as abusing laxatives, throwing up, or exercising excessively.

• *Binge-Eating Disorder:* Recurrent periods of uncontrollably high food intake without associated purge.

These disorders stem from a pervasive fixation with food, weight, and one's physical appearance. An unhealthy connection with food is developed by people who suffer from eating disorders as a coping method for underlying mental pain, poor self-esteem, or a skewed perception of their bodies.

The Relationship Between Impulsivity and Potential Misdiagnosis Traps

Impulsivity is a sign of BPD and eating disorders alike. Impulsive eating habits that are similar to those of an eating disorder can be seen in people with BPD. For example, they can have periods of binge eating to deal with strong negative feelings. But there's an important difference in how severe, common, and widespread these behaviors are. A person's disordered eating habits must satisfy certain requirements listed in the Diagnostic and Statistical Manual of Mental Disorders (DSM-V) for them to be diagnosed with an eating disorder.

Below is a summary of the main distinctions:

Eating disorder:

• *Pervasiveness:* Thoughts and everyday activities are dominated by eating disorder behaviors.

• *Severity:* The excessive behaviors associated with eating disorders can have serious health repercussions.

• *Frequency:* The actions associated with eating disorders happen often and develop into established habits.

• *Focus:* Food, body image, and weight are the main areas of attention.

BPD:

• *Impulsive habits:* Impulsive eating habits might happen during moments of emotional dysregulation.

• *Severity:* Although eating habits might be strong, they are not always as serious or potentially fatal as eating disorders.

• *Frequency*: Unlike eating disorders, eating habits can be episodic rather than constant.

• *Focus:* The focus is more comprehensive, including relational issues, emotional dysregulation, and impulsivity in a variety of contexts.

The Value of an Extensive Assessment

A comprehensive assessment by a mental health specialist is necessary to distinguish BPD from an eating problem. The assessment can include the following:

• *Clinical Interviews:* thorough explanation of the person's medical history, symptoms, and experiences.

• *Psychological Testing:* Standardized tests to evaluate personality characteristics, emotional states, and eating problem behaviors.

• *Physical Examination:* Evaluation of general physical well-being and any issues arising from dietary habits.

Somatic Symptom Disorder (formerly Somatization Disorder)

For those who experience Somatic Symptom Disorder (SSD), formerly known as Somatization Disorder, as well as medical experts seeking to identify it, it can be a perplexing condition. The physical symptoms of SSD are characterized by their persistence and discomfort, which makes them difficult to adequately explain by a disease or underlying illness. These symptoms can cause great anguish and impairment since they can be quite genuine and have a substantial influence on a person's daily life. Shortness of breath, exhaustion, digestive problems, dizziness, and persistent pain are typical examples.

However, impulsivity, trouble sustaining stable relationships, and a widespread pattern of emotional dysregulation are the hallmarks of Borderline Personality Disorder (BPD). Despite their apparent disconnection, BPD can sometimes present with symptoms similar to this medical illnesses, making diagnosis difficult. This is where BPD's idea of dissociation is useful.

Dissociation and the Mind-Body Connection in BPD

A person who dissociates mentally from their ideas, emotions, memories, or sense of self is said to be doing so. There is a range between moderate daydreaming and more extreme sensations such as feeling cut off from one's body or surroundings. Dissociation in BPD can take many forms, and turning emotional discomfort into physical symptoms is one of them. Imagine that a person suffering from BPD is very agitated or anxious. Their mind can inadvertently translate this emotional upheaval into a bodily sensation, such as a knotted stomach or a tightness in the chest, rather than confronting and processing these feelings. Somatization is a phenomenon that can be quite convincing, making people with BPD think they are physically unwell.

Differential Diagnosis's Challenge

Accurate diagnosis might be challenging since dissociative symptoms of BPD and SSD overlap. Both disorders manifest as inexplicable physical symptoms that can seriously disturb everyday living and create great suffering. But there are important differences to take into account:

• ***Emphasis on Distress:*** When it comes to SSD, the physical symptoms are the main emphasis. People are focused on their physical experiences and are always looking for medical care and comfort.

• ***Emotional Correlates: Although*** emotional distress can be present in both diseases, BPD patients often experience physical symptoms in reaction to strong emotions or stressful interpersonal situations. Knowing when to distinguish between the two can be aided by recognizing emotional changes and triggers.

• ***Medical Workup:*** It is essential to do a complete medical assessment. Extensive medical testing can not identify a physical reason for the symptoms in SSD patients. On the other hand, while a physical ailment can exist in some instances of BPD, it would not account for the intensity and duration of the symptoms.

• ***Psychological Assessment:*** A mental health assessment can assist in determining how well an individual can regulate their emotions, interact with others, and dissociate. This can provide important information about whether the physical symptoms are due to mental disturbance, as in the case of borderline personality disorder.

The Way to Successful Therapy

Appropriate therapy can only be implemented after a precise diagnosis. Cognitive behavioral therapy (CBT) is a very successful intervention for SSD. With the help of cognitive behavioral therapy (CBT), people can learn to recognize and question the harmful ideas and attitudes that fuel their health concerns and concentrate on the mistaken physical symptoms. Practicing mindfulness and relaxation methods can also help with physical symptom management.

Dialectical behavior therapy, or DBT, is the gold standard of care for people with BPD. Emotional control, distress tolerance, mindfulness, and interpersonal communication are all important abilities that DBT teaches. People with BPD can lessen the frequency and severity of dissociative episodes, including those that show physical symptoms, by establishing healthy coping mechanisms for their emotions.

Overcoming the Prognosis

It can be very difficult and isolated to live with bodily ailments that have no explanation. A person's well-being can be greatly impacted by both BPD and SSD. However, people can learn to control their symptoms and enhance their quality of life with a correct diagnosis and suitable therapy. Reducing health concerns and improving coping strategies for handling bodily sensations can be part of this for SSD sufferers. It might include learning more effective techniques to control their emotions and forge closer bonds with those who have BPD. Everybody's road to recovery is unique, but with the correct care and guidance, people can overcome these obstacles and learn to lead happy, purposeful lives.

Attention-Deficit/Hyperactivity Disorder (ADHD)

Due to comparable symptoms including emotional dysregulation and impulsivity, borderline personality disorder (BPD) and attention-deficit/hyperactivity disorder (ADHD) can sometimes be misunderstood. However, a deeper examination shows important distinctions between these illnesses' underlying origins, triggers, and symptoms.

ADHD: A Disturbance in Neurodevelopment

One of the most prevalent neurodevelopmental diseases, ADHD is generally identified in infancy and often lingers into adulthood. Dopamine abnormalities in the brain and issues with executive function are its defining characteristics. Individuals with ADHD might display:

• *Inattention:* Being easily sidetracked, having trouble concentrating, being forgetful.

• *Hyperactivity:* Intense physical movement, agitation, and trouble staying still.

• *Impulsivity:* Behaving impulsively, having trouble waiting their time, and speaking without thinking.

These difficulties result from basic variations in the composition and function of the brain's neurotransmitters. Due to a disruption in the reward system caused by dopamine insufficiency in ADHD brains, individuals have persistent cravings for novelty and difficulty with repeated activities. Moreover, differences in the dimensions and organization of the areas responsible for making decisions can lead to increased impulsivity.

BPD: An Emotionally Dysregulated Pattern

In contrast, impulsivity, trouble sustaining good relationships, and a widespread pattern of emotional instability are traits of borderline personality disorder. Basic characteristics of BPD include:

• *Emotional dysregulation:* intense feelings that change quickly, as well as trouble managing emotional reactions.

• *Fear of Abandonment:* An ingrained phobia of being abandoned or rejected, which manifests as pushy or clinging behavior in interpersonal interactions.

• *Instable Relationships:* Unhealthy coping strategies and emotional instability make it difficult to establish and maintain stable, healthy relationships.

• *Compulsive Behaviors:* Taking action without thinking through the consequences, usually resulting in drug misuse, reckless driving, or self-harm.

Emotional Dysregulation: A Complicated Issue

Emotional dysregulation is a feature of both BPD and ADHD, although the causes and triggers are different.

ADHD: Impatience and the need for rapid reward are often connected to impulsivity and emotional outbursts in ADHD. They suffer from delayed pleasure and a continual desire for stimulation, which can lead them to fidget, interrupt conversations, or blurt things out.

BPD: The dread of being abandoned is the root cause of emotional dysregulation in BPD. In the early stages of a relationship, they could idealize someone, but they soon become wary or irate, driving the other person away out of fear of being abandoned. Their relationships become unstable as a result of this "push-pull" dynamic.

Relationship Stress: Distinct Origins, Comparable Results

Relationship difficulties can arise for both BPD and ADHD sufferers, but the fundamental causes are different.

BPD: Unstable relationships are fueled by the fear of abandonment in BPD. Their strong feelings, sensitivity, and paranoia can make for a tense atmosphere that often results in breakups. They could experience severe self-loathing and impulsivity after a breakup.

ADHD: People with ADHD often struggle in relationships because of their inability to focus, forget things, and manage their time well. Couples can get tense as a result of their seeming disinterest or forgetting crucial dates. Relationship financial hardship can also result from reckless conduct or impulsive spending.

The Value of Precise Diagnosis

Making the distinction between BPD and ADHD is essential to creating a successful treatment strategy. Although impulsivity and emotional dysregulation are shared, there are important differences in the underlying causes and triggers of each.

Treatment for ADHD: Usually involves a mix of pharmaceutical control (to control dopamine) and psychotherapy techniques such as cognitive behavioral therapy (CBT) to enhance concentration, planning, and emotional control.

Treatment for Borderline Personality Disorder (BPD): Usually involves psychotherapy techniques such as dialectical behavior therapy (DBT), which teaches patients how to control their emotions, tolerate discomfort, be attentive, and communicate with others.

Mental health practitioners are better able to diagnose patients with more accuracy and provide individualized treatment strategies by being aware of the distinctive characteristics of each disorder. This gives individuals the ability to better control their symptoms, form wholesome connections, and enhance their general well-being.

The Challenge of Differential Diagnosis

Diagnosis of BPD and its associated illnesses can be difficult because of their complicated and overlapping symptoms. It is crucial to get a comprehensive mental health assessment performed by a licensed practitioner with knowledge of personality disorders. To get a precise diagnosis, the examination will include a thorough history, a discussion of the symptoms, and psychiatric tests.

Multimodal therapy is necessary for BPD and associated comorbidities to be effectively managed. The following are some crucial tactics:

Treatment for Dialectical Behavior (DBT): DBT is a very successful treatment that was created especially for BPD. It gives people the tools they need to better communicate, control their emotions, withstand discomfort, and form wholesome relationships. These abilities are essential for handling the impulsivity, emotional dysregulation, and interpersonal connection issues that are often present in BPD.

Trauma-Specific Treatment: Healing requires investigating and processing prior trauma, particularly when trauma is thought to have had a role in the development of BPD. People who are seeking assistance in comprehending how their prior experiences can be influencing their current feelings and actions might benefit from therapies such as Trauma-Focused Cognitive Behavioral Therapy (TF-CBT).

Medicine: Although medicine cannot treat borderline personality disorder (BPD), it can help manage some of the symptoms of related disorders like anxiety or depression. In addition to therapy, antidepressants, mood stabilizers, and anxiety drugs can be utilized to give a more thorough course of treatment.

The Value of an Adoptive Treatment Group: To effectively treat BPD and associated comorbidities, a team approach is often used. A psychiatrist, psychologist, therapist, can be case manager or social worker might be on this team. When these specialists work together, complete treatment that takes into account every facet of the patient's mental health requirements is ensured. Whereas the psychiatrist writes prescriptions for medication when necessary, the therapist offers individual treatment. Practical concerns such as housing, jobs, or establishing connections with support organizations can be handled by the social worker or case manager.

Tailored Care: It's important to keep in mind that each person has a distinct experience. Each person's unique demands and problems will be taken into account while creating their personalized treatment plan. While group treatment can be beneficial for some people, individual therapy can be more beneficial for others. Together, the patient and the therapist will create a treatment plan that is encouraging, safe, and successful.

Stereotypes and stigma: The stigma associated with BPD and several comorbid illnesses, such as DID, can make it difficult for people to get treatment. Dispelling these myths and highlighting the fact that BPD is a curable disorder is crucial. For those with

BPD, there are many tools available to support them in leading happy and purposeful lives.

It takes time, dedication, and self-compassion to heal from BPD and its concomitant illnesses. There will be obstacles along the path, but people with BPD can develop resilience and design a more rewarding future with continued support and dedication to recovery. Recall that you are not alone yourself. There is hope for a better future and assistance accessible.

As we've seen, Borderline Personality Disorder (BPD) is a complicated illness that can have its origins in a combination of environmental variables, genetic predisposition, and early trauma. These underlying factors can show up in many different ways and have a big influence on day-to-day living. I am a therapist who specializes in treating individuals with Borderline Personality Disorder (BPD), therefore I am aware of the difficulties you deal with daily. All of these experiences—the strong feelings, the worry about being abandoned, the difficulty navigating relationships—are real. The good news is that BPD is curable. You can develop a strong sense of self, emotionally stable connections, and a life full of healthy relationships while also learning effective coping mechanisms for your symptoms.

The gold-standard treatment for borderline personality disorder (BPD), dialectical behavior therapy (DBT), will be covered in detail in the next chapter. Think of DBT as your toolbox, a set of abilities you can use to overcome obstacles in life and foster emotional health. The main ideas of DBT will be discussed, including emotional regulation, mindfulness, distress tolerance, and interpersonal effectiveness. These abilities complement one another to provide a thorough foundation for controlling BPD symptoms and promoting a more satisfying existence. Never forget that you are not traveling alone. DBT gives you the tools you need to take charge of your feelings, forge healthy connections with others, and design a life that fulfills you. Now let's get started and begin assembling your BPD toolset.

CHAPTER 4

Dialectical Behavior Therapy (DBT): A Powerful Approach

Managing emotions and relationships can be difficult for those with borderline personality disorder (BPD). Thankfully, dialectical behavior therapy (DBT) is a very successful therapeutic strategy. DBT, as it is often called, has the potential to significantly transform lives. Consider DBT as your own personal toolkit. It's brimming with techniques you can use to regulate those big feelings, strengthen your bonds with others, and feel more in charge of your life.

We're going to open that toolbox and examine the tools within this chapter. We'll discuss topics like emotional regulation, which is all about learning to control those strong emotions healthily, and mindfulness, which assists you in being present in the moment. We'll also cover interpersonal effectiveness, which supports the development and maintenance of wholesome relationships, and distress tolerance, which gives you the tools to deal with difficult circumstances without being overwhelmed. Let us start by going over the fundamental ideas of DBT and how they might support you in your quest for emotional well-being.

Core Concepts of DBT

You can come across dialectical behavior therapy (DBT) if you're trying to learn more about Borderline Personality Disorder (BPD) and the potential treatments. While there are some approaches that both DBT and Cognitive Behavioral Therapy (CBT) use, it's important to understand that DBT provides a more thorough and sophisticated approach that is specially tailored to address the intricacies of BPD. A kind of psychotherapy called dialectical behavior therapy (DBT) is intended especially for people with borderline personality disorder (BPD).

Although there are some approaches that DBT and CBT overlap, a closer examination uncovers significant philosophical differences between them. CBT is often protocol-driven, which means that therapists adhere to a set of guidelines for dealing with certain problems. Consider cognitive behavioral therapy (CBT) as a toolbox with specific skills for every issue. To treat unfavorable thinking patterns linked to social anxiety, for instance, a therapist can use cognitive restructuring approaches. DBT, on the other hand, is a principle-driven treatment. Core principles provide therapists with additional freedom in customizing therapy to meet your requirements. Consider DBT as a tool and material-rich workshop. Serving as your guide, the therapist can modify these methods and tools to develop a customized strategy that targets your unique difficulties.

Important Principles that set DBT Different from CBT

Authentication: This idea recognizes the value of your feelings, experiences, and viewpoints. Your therapist builds a collaborative and trusting environment by providing a secure area where you feel heard and understood. For people with BPD, who often experience strong emotions and battle with feelings of invalidation from others, this validation is essential.

Dialectical Thinking (DBT): DBT acknowledges the complexity of life's paradoxes. Thinking dialectically enables one to simultaneously hold incompatible facts. You can, for instance, establish appropriate coping mechanisms for your emotions while still acknowledging and accepting them. The capacity to maintain many points of view is crucial for managing the difficulties associated with Borderline Personality Disorder (BPD) since sufferers can encounter abrupt mood changes and strong emotions.

Transition and Acknowledgment: As was previously noted, DBT employs two strategies, while CBT focuses on altering maladaptive thought processes. It acknowledges the legitimacy of your present difficulties while also giving you the tools you need to deal with them head-on. This encourages self-compassion, which enables you to approach change with empowerment instead of self-criticism.

Effectiveness of the Therapist: The foundation of DBT is the therapeutic alliance. To establish trust and provide a safe space for you to feel comfortable discussing your vulnerabilities, your therapist works to develop a sincere relationship with you. This solid partnership turns into an effective instrument to help you on your development path. To model appropriate communication and emotional expression, DBT therapists often use self-disclosure, a tactic not commonly seen in CBT.

These fundamental ideas provide therapists the ability to tailor a treatment plan that is both adaptable and focused on your unique requirements. In contrast to the standardized protocols of CBT, which can be less flexible to the intricate and sometimes multidimensional character of BPD, this enables a more comprehensive approach.

The Diverse DBT Approach

Unlike CBT, which primarily relies on individual treatment, DBT provides a multimodal approach via four unique modes:

Individual Therapy: This offers a secure setting where you can examine your feelings, recognize triggers, and put the group therapy techniques into practice. Your therapist acts as a helpful mentor, assisting you in overcoming obstacles and creating useful coping techniques. Together, you will also develop objectives and monitor your progress as therapy progresses.

Skills Group: In a skills group, you will study and put the fundamental DBT techniques into practice with other people who also have BPD. You can exchange your experiences and get insightful knowledge in this encouraging and affirming setting. You'll gain from the distinct viewpoint of others on a similar path while refining your skills in mindfulness, distress tolerance, emotional regulation, and interpersonal effectiveness.

Telephone Consultation: DBT recognizes that unexpected obstacles will certainly arise in life. You can get help and direction from your therapist over the phone when dealing with challenging circumstances that come up outside of treatment sessions. In the heat of the moment, this real-time support system can be very helpful in averting disasters and encouraging constructive coping strategies.

The Therapy Team: In the background, a group of experts committed to your welfare work with your therapist. Social workers, case managers, and additional therapists can be on this team. Together, they guarantee continuity of treatment, assist your therapist, and give you the finest care possible. This team-based methodology guarantees all-encompassing assistance throughout your expedition.

This multipronged strategy guarantees that you will get assistance and direction in all facets of your life. DBT provides a complete safety net that enables you to overcome obstacles and create a more rewarding life by combining individual treatment, skills training, phone consultations, and the support of a committed team.

Core Skillset Techniques of DBT

In contrast to CBT, which is mostly concerned with cognitive restructuring, DBT gives you a wider variety of abilities to control your emotions, strengthen your bonds with others, and endure discomfort. An examination of the key skills training provided by DBT is as follows:

Mindfulness

Like any other skill, dialectical behavior therapy (DBT) takes time and practice to become proficient in. Even though there's a lot to learn, when you actively work with the approaches yourself, the parts will start to fit together. This takes us to a key DBT component: therapists must practice what they preach. Can you imagine having to teach someone how to rock climb without ever being outside of a ladder? Deep comprehension is necessary for teaching these abilities effectively, and it can only be attained from firsthand experience.

Convincing BPD patients of the benefits of mindfulness is the first challenge in teaching it. It's common for people to voice doubt since treatment sometimes involves unfamiliar concepts. Because of this, it's critical to use understandable and relevant language while customizing your explanations to their unique requirements and preferences.

Cultivating Mindfulness: A Path to Present Moment Awareness

A key component of dialectical behavior therapy (DBT), MINDFULNESS is a complex concept with many different interpretations. The key is to focus on one task at a time, be totally present in the here and now, give it your whole attention, and accept it as it is. I'll explain this idea in detail and look at some approaches to teaching mindfulness to others.

It's beneficial to divide mindfulness into two main parts for customers who are new to it:

1. Awareness

This entails concentrating your attention on the task at hand, whether it be driving, strolling, conversing, or just spending time with your pet. It involves using all of your senses to fully experience the current moment, taking in the sights, sounds, tastes, scents, and physical feelings.

Picture yourself becoming comfy and prepared to examine the current situation with a sharpened sense of awareness. There's no need to reach any certain condition or clear your head. We are just going to focus on what is happening to us right now, in this moment.

Using Your Senses:

• *Sight:* Start by taking note of your surroundings. Are there any particular items that catch your eye? Maybe the hue of the walls, a picture on the bookcase, or even dust particles swaying in the sunlight. Without passing judgment, take note of the colors, textures, and forms.

• *Sound:* At this point, concentrate on what you hear. Are you able to differentiate between distinct sounds? Maybe sounds from outside traffic, computer hum, or even your breathing. Just pay attention to the noises without trying to interpret them.

• *Smell:* Gradually alert yourself to any smells you can pick up on. Is there a subtle perfume of coffee, a whiff of fresh flowers, or something else entirely? Observe the scents without passing judgment, even if they are disagreeable.

• *Taste:* If it's comfortable for you, focus on the flavor that's in your mouth. Is there a flavor that is neutral, like toothpaste, leftover from a previous meal? Just taste it and don't pass judgment.

• *Touch:* At last, focus on your physical experiences. Feel the cloth under your skin, the way your body is positioned, or the room's temperature. Without passing judgment, pay attention to any muscular tension or relaxation.

Bringing Everything Together

Gently accept your ideas as they come to you and then return your focus to your sensory experience. It's similar to a slow dance: acknowledging your thoughts without becoming engrossed in them and bringing your attention back to the here and now.

The following are some strategies for living a more attentive and aware life:

• *Mindful Coffee Break: Take* a few sips of your morning coffee and appreciate its scent, flavor, and warmth in your hands rather than guzzling it down quickly.

• ***Mindful Commute:*** Pay attention to the sights and sounds around you whether you're driving or taking the bus. Take in the shifting landscape, the sounds of passing traffic, and the sensation of the seat under you.

• ***Mindful discussion: Pay*** attention to the words, tone of voice, and facial expressions of the other person throughout a discussion rather than planning your next move.

You can develop more awareness in your daily life by implementing these easy exercises and practical examples. Recall that practicing mindfulness is a necessary skill. Have perseverance and patience. The more you use your senses and concentrate on the here and now, the more mindfulness can help you with emotional regulation and problem-solving.

2. Acceptance

This important—but often disregarded—aspect is expressing your experience without passing judgment. Just recognize your anxiety if you notice it. Be mindful of feelings of "pointlessness" or boredom without passing judgment. Allow yourself to feel your bodily pain without projecting any negative energy onto it. Seeing your experience—thoughts, feelings, and physical sensations—with an open mind and without passing judgment is the essence of mindfulness.

Being mindful involves embracing whatever comes up in the moment, both good and bad, in addition to concentrating on the here and now. It can be difficult to accept this as our brains are wired to categorize events as positive, negative, or neutral. On the other hand, you can learn to control your emotions and deal with life's ups and downs by practicing acceptance.

Embrace acceptance in your mindfulness practice by following these tips:

Recognizing Feelings:

• ***Anxiety:*** Let's say you're worried about a presentation you have coming up. Just admit that you're feeling nervous: "Okay, I'm feeling anxious right now." Do not criticize yourself psychologically for experiencing anxiety. By acknowledging it, even just a little, you can distance yourself from the feeling and examine it objectively.

• ***Boredom:*** When you're forced to wait in line, you start to become bored. Observe your ennui without passing judgment. Recognize your boredom without mentally judging yourself by saying, "This is boring, but that's okay." You can keep boredom from turning into anger or irritation by learning to tolerate it.

• *Anger:* When you're stuck in traffic, you feel a surge of rage. Declare, "A surge of anger is coming up," to acknowledge the anger. While it's okay to feel upset, resist allowing your rage to rule you. Make use of this understanding to choose a more thoughtful course of action, such as inhaling deeply and allowing the anger to subside.

• *Sadness:* Sadness can sometimes strike seemingly out of nowhere. Say, "There's a wave of sadness washing over me right now," to acknowledge your sadness. Permit yourself to feel the grief without passing judgment. Recall that melancholy is a common human feeling, and learning to accept it can help you deal with it and go on.

• *Grief:* Coping with a loss is a normal and difficult process. Healing from sorrow requires accepting its suffering. Say to yourself, "I'm feeling the pain of grief right now," to acknowledge your loss. Permit yourself to experience anger, sorrow, and other grief-related emotions. Although the suffering won't go away quickly, accepting it can guide you through the mourning process.

Acknowledging Physical Sensations:

Uncomfortable: Perhaps tension has caused a knot to form tightly in your shoulders. Instead of tightening up even more, focus on the feeling in your body. Without passing judgment, acknowledge the tension by saying, "I feel tight in my shoulders." You can be able to let go of the physical strain that comes with stress by accepting this.

Pain: Suffering from chronic pain can be quite frustrating. Even though the pain can not go away completely, acknowledging it can be a useful strategy. Recognize the suffering without passing judgment: "I'm in pain right now." This acceptance lessens the emotional burden of the pain itself and frees you up to concentrate on coping strategies.

Here are some real-world instances of how to use acceptance in your mindfulness exercises:

• *Gridlock:* Are you caught in a gridlock? Breathe deeply and admit your dissatisfaction. Recognize that you have no control over the circumstance and direct your attention to things you can manage, like breathing or relaxing music.

• ***Error:*** Were you the victim of an error at work? Recognize your emotions—disappointment, shame—but try not to focus on them. Recognize that errors occur, absorb lessons from them, and move on.

• ***Negative Thoughts:*** Everyone sometimes thinks negatively. Just admit them as they occur by saying, "I'm having a negative thought right now." Refocus your attention on the here and now with gentleness, and don't berate yourself for thinking the idea.

You can change the way you interact with your ideas and feelings by engaging in acceptance practices. You'll have the ability to see them objectively, which will enable you to react to them more thoughtfully and creatively. Recall that acceptance only entails accepting your experience for what it is, without any further negativity. It does not require endorsing negative. You'll develop more calm and clarity in your daily life the more you practice accepting your experiences.

Preventing Illusions: Reinterpreting Religion and "Meditation"

Avoid using words that might lead to misunderstandings while promoting mindfulness. Here are some things to remember:

Practice meditation: Many individuals mistakenly believe that "mindfulness" and "meditation" are synonymous words. Although they are related, several important differences might help your clients understand mindfulness better. Think of mindfulness as a skill that you can use every day. It involves focusing your attention on the here and now and objectively observing your feelings, ideas, and physical experiences. It is comparable to a mental muscle that can be developed with repetition. Consider meditation as a particular practice that you might engage in to develop awareness. It usually entails sitting quietly and concentrating on a single point of awareness, such as your breathing, a mantra—a word or sound that is repeated—or even a bodily experience.

This is why it is important to make this distinction:

Preconceptions: For novices, the term "meditation" can evoke visions of spending hours upon hours sitting in lotus posture, which can be frightening.

Put Practice First: By highlighting the useful components of mindfulness, such as being present in the moment, you take away the burden of adopting a certain posture or mental state.

Increasing Accessibility to Mindfulness

The following are some strategies to help you become more mindful:

In a nutshell: To ease yourself into the practice, start with brief mindfulness activities that take just a few minutes.

• ***Daily Activities:*** Make mindfulness a part of your regular schedules. Take note of the sensation of your feet hitting the floor when you walk, the flavor of your food when you eat, or the sound of your breathing as you go off to sleep.

• ***Body Scans:*** Lead yourself in a body scan meditation in which you can concentrate on various body regions and pay attention to whatever feelings you experience without passing judgment.

• ***Mindful Movement:*** Learn about mindful movement techniques that include physical exercise and mindfulness, such as tai chi or mild yoga.

Regardless of their prior beliefs about meditation, you can assist anybody build a feeling of mindfulness that works for them by emphasizing the fundamentals of present-moment awareness and providing a variety of practice options.

Religion: While mindfulness is a useful technique for controlling emotions and developing present-moment awareness, several myths need to be cleared up. This is a summary of the relationship between mindfulness and religion:

Origins of Traditional Knowledge

Eastern practices like Zen Buddhism are indeed the origins of mindfulness. These traditions placed a strong emphasis on meditation techniques meant to develop inner serenity and present-moment awareness. But the fundamental idea of mindfulness, which is to pay attention to the present moment without passing judgment, applies to everyone. No matter one's creed, it transcends particular religious ideas and is accessible to everybody.

Put the Benefits of Practice First:

As Therapists, it's important to keep the advantages of mindfulness for persons with BPD front and center while teaching them. Emphasize the benefits of mindfulness for them:

• Control anxiety and tension

• Boost attention and concentration

• Raise self-awareness

• Strengthen emotional control

If they bring up religion while discussing mindfulness, you might explain that the practice is secular and accept their point of view. As an example, consider this:

That's a thought-provoking point. Although certain religious traditions are the source of mindfulness, anybody can benefit from the fundamental practice of being in the present moment, regardless of their own beliefs." You can make sure that clients from various backgrounds feel comfortable studying mindfulness as a tool for personal improvement by maintaining a neutral and respectful attitude.

Illustrations of Reframing

The following are some approaches to reinterpret mindfulness ideas such that they are more broadly applicable:

- Alternative to: "Mindfulness meditation" try: "Mindfulness practice" or even "Focusing on the present moment"
- Try "developing greater self-awareness" or "cultivating inner peace" in place of the Buddhist idea of "achieving enlightenment"

Regardless of their religious views, you can enable your customers to accept mindfulness as a useful technique for improving their well-being by highlighting the practical advantages and taking an impartial stance.

Mindfulness Flexibility: Crafting Solutions for Diverse Situations

After gaining a fundamental grasp of mindfulness, the next stage is to tailor its application to the individual's objectives. This is how you "personalize" mindfulness in an effective way:

Determine the Target Behaviors: Do you ever find yourself thinking back on previous transgressions or worried about the future all the time? Although these are typical occurrences, they can be cognitively taxing and keep you from experiencing the present. A potent method for escaping these counterproductive thought habits is mindfulness. Consider the issues you want to resolve. Do you find it difficult to stop worrying too much about the future or dwelling too much on the past? Emphasize how practicing mindfulness can assist them in escaping these destructive thought patterns.

Finding the precise mental patterns that are preventing your forward motion is the first step. Here are a few typical instances:

• ***Rumination:*** Do you find yourself thinking back on previous experiences and focusing on regrets or mistakes?

• ***Worry:*** Are you prone to worrying about the worst-case situations and imagining issues down the road?

• ***Negative Self-Talk:*** Are you continuously pushed down by a critical inner voice?

It's not mindfulness that requires you to push these ideas away. It's more important to acknowledge them without passing judgment. How it can assist is as follows:

Enhanced Awareness: You can increase your awareness of your ideas as they come to you by engaging in mindfulness practices. This enables you to see them without being entangled in them.

Non-Judgmental Observation: Mindfulness enables you to recognize your thoughts without passing judgment, much like clouds moving above the sky. You can identify them as "thoughts" only, not as facts.

Reorienting Yourself: You have the option to gently return your attention to the here and now when you become aware of an unhelpful thinking habit. This might be paying attention to your breathing, your environment, or a bodily experience.

Practical Illustrations:

Thinking back: Feeling irritated and agitated, you're mentally reliving a recent dispute. When you practice mindfulness, you become aware of these thoughts as they arise and upset you. You choose to quiet your body and mind by focusing on your breathing while accepting them without passing judgment.

Concern: You're thinking about all the possible things that can go wrong with an impending presentation. Being attentive helps you acknowledge your concern and its effects. To control your anxiousness, you then decide to concentrate on your current activities, such as making notes or doing deep breathing exercises.

Negative self-talk: You are told you're not good enough by a critical voice. Being attentive allows you to notice the idea for what it is—just a thought, not your whole identity—and to watch it without passing judgment. After that, you have the option of concentrating on your virtues or self-compassion exercises.

Shifting Time Perspective: We've all had the sensation of being trapped in the past, replaying a fight, or living in constant concern about a presentation that's coming up. These kinds of thinking can be emotionally taxing and deprive us of our present-day agency.

The truth is that practicing mindfulness can assist you in changing your perspective on time and refocusing your attention on the here and now. Dwelling on the past or the future is often motivated by certain feelings. Here's how to recognize these relationships:

Past-Oriented Thinking:

- Thinking back on a lost chance can make you feel frustrated or disappointed.
- Reliving a previous dispute could make you feel sad, angry, or regretful.

Future-Oriented Thinking:

- Anxiety or tension can arise from worrying about a job interview.
- Phantasies of the worst-case might make one feel insecure or afraid.

Real-Life Examples:

Breakup blues: You're depressed and furious, and you can't stop thinking about a recent split. This prevents you from going on with your life and taking pleasure in the things you used to love to do.

Nervousness at a job interview: You can't stop fretting about your impending job interview and all the possible outcomes. It's challenging to focus on interview preparation because of this nervousness.

Shifting Your Focus:

You can witness these feelings and ideas without passing judgment by practicing mindfulness. Awareness leads to choosing:

• ***Identify the Trigger:*** Take note of the emotional reaction and the related cognitive pattern (worrying about the future or focusing on the past).

• *Non-judgmental Observation:* Recognize these emotions and ideas without being sucked into them.

• *Shift to Present Moment:* Return your focus to the here and now with gentle guidance. To ground yourself, pay attention to your breathing, your environment, or a bodily feeling.

Through engaging in mindfulness practices, you can discover ways to overcome these emotional patterns. This enables you to:

• *Handle Tough Emotions: You* can recognize your feelings without giving them power over you.

• *Concentrate on What Counts:* Your focus moves from wishful thinking to experiences and activities in the here and now.

• *Develop Resilience:* You become stronger at overcoming obstacles and navigating the ups and downs of life.

Recall that practicing mindfulness is a necessary skill. It will become simpler to change your attention and find calm in the here and now as you continue to practice mindfulness.

3. The Present's Power

Imagine bearing the burden of a previous event on your back in the form of a hefty rucksack. It can be an unpleasant disagreement, a failure on a personal level, or even a distressing childhood memory. Weighing that weight down would be freeing, wouldn't it? By assisting you in concentrating on the here and now, mindfulness enables you to achieve just that. Ignoring difficulties is not the same as living completely in the moment. There will be painful and challenging moments in life since life can be unpredictable. The way you approach such times makes all the difference. Reminiscing on the past makes us practically carry that burden around.

Think about this:

• Something unpleasant happens to you (for example, a nasty fight with a loved one).

• The emotional effect increases if you keep thinking back on it and reliving the feelings from the past. The past begins to eclipse the present.

The Capacity of Mindfulness

You can more easily navigate the present with the aid of mindfulness. How to do it is as follows:

• *Being Here Now:* Mindfulness allows you to notice previous events while focusing on the present. Even though you can be upset or angry about the disagreement, you have the power to deal with those feelings in a healthy way.

• *Acceptance and Self-Compassion:* Despite its challenges, mindfulness promotes acceptance of the current moment. This is acknowledging your prior wounds and permitting yourself to be compassionate with yourself, not endorsing the past incident.

• *Mindful Action:* By being in the moment, you can consider how to use your abilities and resources to handle the circumstance. You can decide to concentrate on moving on constructively by having a cool-headed and straightforward discussion with the individual you fought with.

Real-World Illustration:

Let's revisit the hurtful argument. When you practice mindfulness, you accept the pain as it is and think about how it could be hurting you. Choosing self-compassion means accepting that everyone errs from time to time. Next, you investigate how to have a productive conversation with the individual in question, keeping your attention on the current circumstance and your potential for a successful outcome. By using this attitude, you can stop being burdened by the past and instead control your current sensations, which are suffering multiplied by one. Maintaining present-moment awareness is simpler the more you practice mindfulness. This enables you to:

• *Deal with Difficulties More Effectively:* You can better handle challenging emotions and react to circumstances by keeping your attention on the here and now.

• *Savor Happy Moments:* Being mindful improves your capacity to completely recognize and cherish the happy times that are now occurring.

• *Accept life as a journey:* Good and unpleasant events abound in life. You can experience them all more deliberately and avoid being paralyzed by the past or the future by practicing mindfulness.

Distress Tolerance

Life throws natural curveballs, and BPD can make managing these challenges particularly difficult. DBT gives you distress tolerance skills to handle strong feelings without turning to dangerous coping strategies like self-harm or drug abuse. These skills include avoidance methods, self-soothing strategies, and building your tolerance for uncomfortable feelings.

When strong feelings hit, keeping things under control can feel difficult. People dealing with disasters might turn to bad habits to cope. But there are ways to handle these times successfully. This part discusses two key DBT (Dialectical Behavior Therapy) tactics for surviving a crisis without turning to harmful actions:

Cost-Benefit Analysis: This method helps you carefully analyze the effects of your activities.

RESISTT Skills: These are a set of techniques for controlling emotions and staying present during emotional pain.

The first step is recognizing the unhealthy ways you might respond during a disaster. This could include drug abuse, self-harm, distancing yourself, or acting irresponsibly.

Cost-Benefit Analysis: Weighing Your Options

Imagine a situation where you're tempted to use a bad coping strategy. A cost-benefit study helps you see the bigger picture. Often, the instant comfort these behaviors offer can hide their long-term negative effects.

The Cost-Benefit Analysis Worksheet:

This paper (you can find examples online) walks you through finding both the good and bad results associated with your chosen behavior, and those of withdrawing from it. Here's the process:

• *Benefits and Costs of Your Behavior:* List the instant good feelings or benefits you associate with the behavior and the bad effects it might bring in the long run.

• *Benefits and Costs of Staying Calm:* Consider the possible positive results of not turning to bad behavior. Are there possible downsides to fighting the urge (like brief discomfort)?

• ***Rating the Impact:*** Once you've found both sides, give a number value (1-5) to each based on its perceived worth. This helps you to move beyond simply counting things and gives a more weighted analysis.

Benefits of Cost-Benefit Analysis

• ***Increased Awareness:*** You gain a larger viewpoint, showing the full range of effects connected with your behavior.

• ***Empowered Decision-Making:*** By clearly weighing the costs and rewards, you can make informed choices about your actions at the moment.

• ***Motivation for Change:*** Seeing the bad effects in sharp contrast to the possible benefits of healthy choices can inspire you to seek change.

RESISTT Skills: Managing the Urge

Even with the best goals, changing established habits takes time and practice. Here are the RESISTT skills to help you control urges and stay present during emotional distress:

R: Reframe:

This includes changing your viewpoint on the situation. Instead of focusing on bad thoughts, try to find a more fair view. Look for possible silver linings or different meanings.

Imagine feeling overwhelmed by a tough situation. Everything seems bleak, and your feelings threaten to spiral. Here's where reframing comes in – a powerful tool to change your viewpoint and find a more fair view. Reframing generally means changing the way you look at something. It's about finding the silver lining, the secret chance even in a difficult scenario (Linehan, 1993a). The key is to achieve this without reducing the truth of your feelings or minimizing your problems.

Example:

Let's say you've been working hard to control a chronic disease. After months of growth, you suffer a hiccup. Frustrated, you might think: "What's wrong with me? I'll never get this under control!"

OR

You're feeling swamped with anger after a fight. Instead of focusing on the criticism, rethink the situation: "This fight doesn't define my entire relationship. We can communicate better next time."

This is just one example, and the exact reworking will change based on the case.

Here's how rethinking can help:

• *Acknowledge the Difficulty:* First, realize that failures are normal. They don't erase all your past attempts.

• *Compare to the Past:* Think back to where you were before starting this trip. Are you dealing better now, even with this latest hurdle? This shows the work you've done.

• *Shift the Focus:* Instead of focusing on the loss, focus on the skills you've acquired. Can you use these skills to navigate this challenge?

By changing the situation, you can see it as a brief hurdle, not an inevitable loss. This allows you to move forward with a more cheerful attitude.

There are different ways to rethink a situation:

• *Compare to the Past:* Track your progress to see how far you've come.

• *Compare to Others:* While not always ideal, considering someone facing a more important problem can give perspective on your situation. Remember, the goal isn't to lessen their problems but to broaden your viewpoint.

• **Compare to Global Events:** Sometimes, realizing the pain of others facing great challenges can help us understand the relative nature of our problems.

The Power of Self-Talk

The way you talk to yourself plays a key role in forming your feelings. When criticism controls your self-talk, it can worsen mental discomfort. Are you focused on the worst-case scenario? Challenge these thoughts by considering more realistic options. Create personal themes you can repeat during difficult times. Examples include "I can get through this," or "These emotions are intense, but they won't last forever." By building healthy self-talk habits, you can counter negative thoughts and create a more adaptable mindset.

Reframing is a skill that takes practice. The more you use it, the more skilled you become at changing your viewpoint and finding a more balanced view, even in tough scenarios. This fresh view allows you to handle obstacles with greater mental control.

E" of RESISTT: Mindfully Engaging in an Activity

Why Distraction Works:

Imagine feeling overwhelmed by a difficult situation. Researchers (Koole, 2009) tell us that simply trying to suppress unwanted emotions can make them stronger. The key lies in distraction – shifting your focus to something else entirely. Telling yourself "I don't want to feel this way" can backfire. This act of suppression inadvertently strengthens the unwanted emotion. It's like trying to force a beach ball underwater; it just pops back up with more force! The answer lies in mindful distraction. Acknowledge the emotion without judgment, and then gently guide your attention elsewhere. This allows you to move past the emotional storm without getting swept away.

The goal is to have a list of tasks easily available when mental discomfort hits. Here's how to build your toolkit:

• *Brainstorm Activities:* Think about activities that truly grab your attention and hold your interest. This could include anything from going for a walk or calling a friend to baking cookies or playing with a pet.

• *Start a List:* Begin making your list during a calm time. You can find motivation online or from personal events.

• *Expand Your choices:* Regularly add new activities to your list. The more choices you have, the better ready you'll be to handle different scenarios.

• *Prioritize Length:* Aim for a long list. The more choices you have, the easier it will be to find something that effectively stops you in the moment.

The goal is to find things that truly grab your attention and help you separate from the mental turmoil.

There's no "one size fits all" answer. Experiment and find what works best for you.

"S" of RESISTT – Doing Something for Someone Else

When a crisis hits, the desire to hide and become self-absorbed is reasonable. However, helping others can be a surprisingly effective way to break free from this cycle of negativity. By moving your attention outwards and focusing on the needs of someone else, you achieve several things:

Distraction: The act of helping someone else occupies your mind, offering a temporary respite from your worries. Imagine baking a comforting casserole for a sick friend. The process of gathering ingredients, following a recipe, and the satisfaction of creating something nourishing can take you outside your emotional storm.

Connection: Helping strengthens the bonds you share with others. Performing an act of kindness fosters a sense of connection and belonging, which can be especially comforting during difficult times. The simple act of visiting a lonely neighbor or volunteering at a local animal shelter can create a sense of purpose and social connection.

Perspective: Helping those facing even greater challenges can offer a fresh perspective on your situation. Volunteering at a soup kitchen or homeless shelter can expose you to the struggles of others. Witnessing their resilience can inspire you to approach your challenges with renewed strength and appreciation for what you have.

To successfully utilize this strategy, it's helpful to have a pre-built "helper toolkit" filled with ideas for helping others. Here's how to build yours:

Brainstorm Acts of Kindness: Consider activities that align with your interests and skills. Do you enjoy baking? Perhaps offering to whip up a batch of cookies for a busy colleague. Are you a whiz with technology? Maybe you can help an older relative learn how to use video chat to connect with loved ones.

Create a List: Compile your thoughts into an easily available list. This could be a real notebook you carry with you, a note on your phone, or even a digital document on your computer.

Consider Feasibility: Be realistic about the time and energy you have available during a crisis. Offering to help a friend move across town might not be the best choice if you're hurting yourself. However, running errands or picking up food can be a doable and helpful gift.

Prioritize Safety: The act of helping should be safe for both you and the receiver of your assistance. For instance, if you're not comfortable giving childcare, there are other ways to support a friend with young children, such as making a meal or offering to help with cleaning.

Helping others can be a double-edged sword. While it can be a powerful tool for managing emotional distress, it's crucial to consider your limitations. For example, if you're experiencing suicidal thoughts, offering to babysit a friend's children might not be the wisest course of action. It's important to prioritize your well-being while still striving to connect with others. Discuss these factors with a trusted friend, family member, or mental health professional. Together, you can develop a safe and effective approach to using this skill during difficult times. They can help you brainstorm appropriate ways to help others while ensuring your well-being remains a priority.

By incorporating "Doing Something for Someone Else" into your emotional management toolkit, you gain a powerful tool to navigate emotional distress. It allows you to step outside your troubles, connect with others, and gain a renewed perspective on your challenges. Remember, even small acts of kindness can have a ripple effect, fostering a sense of connection and positivity in yourself and those around you.

The "I" of RESISTT: Intense Sensations

This idea might seem odd, but study shows it can be a powerful distraction method.

Many people struggling with emotional distress resort to self-harm. While this behavior is ultimately destructive, it can offer a reprieve. The intense physical pain serves as a distraction, pulling attention away from overwhelming emotions. The key lies in identifying healthy ways to generate intense physical sensations that provide a similar distraction without the associated harm.

Consider these alternatives:

• *Thermal Extremes:* Take a boiling hot shower or dive into a cold bath. The drastic temperature change can be a powerful jolt to the system, giving a brief escape from mental turmoil.

• *Controlled Pressure:* Hold an ice cube in your hand for a set amount of time. The increasing coldness will intensify, providing a focused sensation that can compete with emotional pain. Alternatively, snap a rubber band against your wrist with moderate force. The sting can be a startling distraction.

• *Sensory Play:* Chew on crushed ice or frozen fruit. The intense cold and odd feel can be a welcome relief, especially for those who find comfort in mouth stimulation.

• *Environmental Extremes:* Go for a quick walk on a scorching day or a chilly evening. The physical pain of hot or cold weather can be a powerful distraction, forcing your mind to focus on the external feeling. Be sure to dress properly and value safety in extreme temps.

• *Sun Exposure (with Caution!):* Lie in the warm sun (with sunscreen!) for a limited time. The warmth on your skin can be a calming and grounding feeling, giving you a short break from mental discomfort.

Building Your Sensory Toolkit

The more choices you have in your toolbox, the better prepared you'll be to handle crisis scenarios. Here's how to build your personal sensory toolkit:

Brainstorm: Think about things that generate strong physical feelings you find acceptable. Consider temperature, pressure, taste, and even proprioception (your body's sense of position and movement).

Create a List: Compile your thoughts into an easily available list. This could be a real notebook, a note on your phone, or even a digital document.

Experiment Safely: Try out different activities to see what works best for you. Start slow and gradually raise the energy as needed, always stressing safety.

Finding healthy ways to manage emotional distress is an ongoing process. The key is to experiment and discover what works best for you. If you find yourself struggling with self-harm or other unhealthy coping mechanisms, don't hesitate to reach out to a trusted friend, family member, or mental health professional for support. By incorporating "Experiencing Intense Sensations" into your emotional management toolkit, you gain a powerful tool to navigate crises. It allows you to shift your focus, offering a temporary respite from overwhelming emotions and empowering you to move forward more healthily. Remember, even small adjustments to your coping mechanisms can have a significant impact on your overall well-being.

The "I" of RESISTT: Shut It Out

There are situations where simply removing yourself physically from the trigger isn't enough. Your thoughts relentlessly replay the problem, preventing you from utilizing your coping skills or accessing your inner sense of calm. This is where the concept of "pushing away" comes in – a Distress Tolerance Skill (Linehan, 1993b) that utilizes your imagination to create a mental distance from the problem.

Before turning to pushing away, it's important to examine the situation. Here's a quick treatment process:

Is it Solvable Now? Can you actively address the problem right now? Do you hold the necessary skills and resources to handle it effectively? If the answer is yes, problem-solving is the most effective course of action. Pushing away simply delays the inevitable.

Is Now the Right Time? Even if a solution exists, consider the time. Are you in a clear and focused state of mind to approach the issue productively? It might be better to postpone facing the problem until you're feeling calmer and more creative.

Pushing Away When Necessary

If both questions point towards the need to postpone dealing with the problem, "pushing away" can offer brief comfort. Here's how to utilize this technique:

Identify the Trigger: Pinpoint the specific problem causing your emotional discomfort. Is it a recent argument? An upcoming deadline? Write it down to solidify it in your mind.

Visualization: The Box Close your eyes and make a clear mental picture reflecting the problem. For instance, if it's a fight with a friend, imagine their face or name.

Containment: Imagine putting this image of the problem inside a strong box. Carefully close the door and secure it with twine or rope. The goal is to convince your mind that the problem is contained and unavailable for the time being.

Mental Storage: Picture yourself putting this sealed box on a high shelf in a metaphorical closet. Lock the closet door and add a symbolic bar or chain for an extra layer of security. This supports the idea that the problem is safely out of sight and out of mind (for now).

Employing Pushing Away Effectively

Sparingly: Use this skill as a last option, after trying other coping strategies like problem-solving or mood control techniques.

Temporarily: The goal is to create a short window of emotional relief, not permanent denial. Schedule a time to return and address the problem later when you're in a calmer state.

Pushing away is a temporary solution, not a permanent fix. Like any technique that involves suppressing thoughts or emotions, it can backfire if used excessively. Overuse can lead to avoidance, making the problem fester and potentially worsen in the long run. By incorporating "pushing away" strategically, you gain a tool to create temporary distance from overwhelming problems. This allows you to utilize your coping skills more effectively and navigate emotional distress more healthily.

The "T" of RESISTT: Think Neutral Thoughts

This idea, a core of Distress Tolerance Skills, might seem odd, but it can be surprisingly effective in lowering the strength of overwhelming feelings and urges.

When emotions run high, our minds tend to fixate on thoughts that fuel the emotional fire. Focusing on neutral thoughts offers a way to break free from this cycle. By directing your attention towards something unrelated to your distress, you create a mental distraction, allowing the intensity of your emotions to subside.

Examples of Neutral Thoughts:

Neutral ideas can be anything that doesn't worsen your emotional state. Here are some ways to add them to your emotional control toolkit:

Mindful Observation: Describe your surroundings objectively. Notice the colors, sizes, and textures of the items around you. Name them quietly in your mind – "desk, chair, window." This simple act of focusing on the present moment can stop the circle of negative thoughts.

Mantras: Repeating a relaxing phrase or mantra can be a powerful tool. Examples include "Peace and calm," "It is what it is," or any phrase that connects with you. The key is to choose something that creates a sense of acceptance and neutrality.

Engaging Activities: Sing a familiar song, repeat a poem, or even count backward from 100. Engaging in a simple, repetitive activity fills your thoughts and provides a cushion from overwhelming feelings.

Spiritual Practices: For some, prayer or meditation can serve as a form of neutral thinking. Focusing on a higher power or inner peace can offer a feeling of calmness and separation from emotional turmoil.

The key to using neutral thoughts effectively lies in personalization. Think about activities or mantras that already bring you a sense of calm. Do you find solace in nature? Perhaps focusing on the sights and sounds of your surroundings can be your go-to neutral thought strategy. Do you have a favorite calming song? Humming or singing silently can be a powerful tool for emotional regulation. Sometimes, we already utilize neutral thoughts without realizing it. Pay attention to your behavior during moments of emotional distress. Do you have a habit of humming a particular tune when feeling overwhelmed? Or perhaps you find yourself unconsciously listing items in your environment. Recognizing these existing behaviors as forms of "focusing on neutral thoughts" empowers you to utilize them more consciously and effectively.

Focusing on neutral thoughts is a temporary strategy for managing emotional distress. It doesn't aim to erase or suppress your emotions. The goal is to create a window of emotional neutrality, allowing you to utilize other coping mechanisms or simply ride out the wave of emotion in a healthier way. By incorporating "focusing on neutral thoughts" into your emotional management toolkit, you gain a valuable tool for navigating emotional storms. It allows you to create a mental buffer from overwhelming emotions, fostering a sense of calm and empowering you to move forward in a more mindful and composed manner.

The "T" of RESISTT: Take a Break

This idea, a cornerstone of Distress Tolerance Skills, might seem easy, but its success lies in its ability to interrupt the emotional storm and make room for more thoughtful action. When emotions run high, our reactions are often impulsive and fueled by the heat of the moment. Taking a break allows you to step back from the immediate situation and gain a more objective perspective. By creating this temporary distance, you're better equipped to navigate the challenge with greater clarity and control.

The idea of "taking a break" can appear in different ways

Physical Breaks: Sometimes, a literal change of scenery is all you need. A brisk walk outside, a quick coffee break at work, or even a short drive can provide a much-needed mental and physical shift. Even a few minutes of fresh air and a change of stance can do wonders for emotional control.

Planned Breaks: Feeling overwhelmed by a looming deadline or a heavy workload? Schedule strategic breaks throughout the day. Use this time for mindful breathing exercises, light stretches, or simply gazing out the window. These mini-breaks can help you recharge and return to your tasks with renewed focus and energy.

Mental Breaks: You don't always need a physical change of pace. Practice mindfulness techniques like meditation or deep breathing exercises. Focusing on your breath or engaging in a guided imagery exercise can effectively transport you to a calmer mental space. Visualize yourself in a peaceful setting, like a calming beach or a serene forest. Engaging your senses in this visualization can create a powerful sense of relaxation.

Strategic Breaks: Taking a break can also involve delegating tasks or prioritizing responsibilities. Feeling stretched thin? Can you ask a colleague for help with a project? Does an errand need to be done today, or can it be rescheduled for a calmer time? Learning to say no and prioritizing self-care is a crucial form of taking a break.

Finding What Works for You

The key to using breaks successfully lies in personalization. Experiment and discover what works best for you. Do a few jumping jacks get your blood moving and clear your head? Perhaps listening to calming music provides a sense of emotional haven. The options are endless.

Breaks: Not Avoidance

It's important to distinguish between taking a break and avoidance. Breaks are temporary respites, allowing you to return to the situation with a more composed approach. Avoidance, on the other hand, involves neglecting or postponing your problems indefinitely. Breaks are most beneficial when used strategically. While they offer a powerful tool for managing emotional distress, taking excessive breaks can disrupt your responsibilities and goals. The aim is to find a healthy balance, incorporating breaks into your routine without hindering your overall progress. It allows you to create a temporary pause, fostering a sense of calm and empowering you to approach challenges with greater clarity and control. Remember, stepping back doesn't mean giving up; it means taking a strategic step toward a more mindful and empowered resolution.

Emotional Regulation

Individuals with BPD often fight to control their feelings successfully. DBT offers tools to spot your feelings, understand their causes, and build healthy ways to share and control them. This includes learning to support your feelings while also building skills to control their strength and length.

Imagine yourself standing on a windy beach, the huge ocean stretching before you. The waves crash and roll, some gentle and playful, others strong and awe-inspiring. Our feelings are much like these waves – ever-present, active, and constantly in change. Emotional control, a cornerstone of mental well-being, allows you to handle this emotional terrain with skill and ease. The first step in successful emotional control includes developing a sense of thoughtful awareness. Imagine yourself standing back from the shore, watching the waves rather than being swept away by them. Similarly, emotional control pushes you to watch your feelings, noticing the physical sensations, thoughts, and urges surrounding them. This objective view helps you to better understand your mental world.

Identifying Your Triggers

Certain events, situations, or even people can act as emotional triggers, typically evoking specific emotional reactions. Through self-reflection and journalling, you can begin to recognize these triggers. Understanding your triggers allows you to predict their possible effect and prepare coping strategies in advance.

Our thoughts significantly impact our mental state. Negative or skewed thinking habits can worsen emotional discomfort. Cognitive retraining, a core concept of emotional control, includes addressing these unhelpful thoughts and replacing them with more balanced and realistic views. For instance, the catastrophizing thought, "This talk is going to be a disaster," can be reframed as, "I'm prepared, and I'll do my best. Even if it's not perfect, it won't be the end of the world." Once you've discovered your triggers and reframed harmful thoughts, you can prepare yourself with a toolbox of methods to handle emotional energy.

However, for people dealing with Borderline Personality Disorder (BPD), standard methods might require extra assistance. This is where Emotion Efficacy Therapy (EET) comes in.

Emotion Efficacy Therapy

We all experience a wide range of feelings throughout our lives. Emotion effectiveness refers to our ability to control these emotions effectively. It includes both our views about our emotional powers and the skills we hold to handle emotional events in a healthy and adaptable way. Individuals with high emotion effectiveness can experience a full range of feelings while still reacting in a way that fits with their values and the demands of the situation.

Think of feeling effectiveness as a two-pronged method. One part includes your views about your ability to control your mental life. Do you view yourself as someone who can weather mental storms? The other part includes the real skills you hold to handle these mental situations. Can you successfully handle difficult feelings, utilize healthy coping strategies, and share your values even when emotions run high? The better your emotional effectiveness, the more skilled you'll be at managing the complexities of your emotional world.

Developing EET, or Emotion Efficacy Therapy, includes a deep study of the factors that affect our connection with feelings. We found key weaknesses and dysfunctional behavioral patterns that can greatly hinder emotional effectiveness.

Common Vulnerabilities:

• ***Biological Predisposition:*** Some people are just born more sensitive. They might feel feelings more strongly than others, kind of like having a built-in emotional level knob set a bit higher. This can make it harder to handle strong feelings.

• ***Emotion Avoidance:*** Efforts to stifle or avoid uncomfortable feelings can become a major barrier. This "experiential avoidance" can prevent you from fully processing and understanding your emotional feelings.

• ***Distress Intolerance:*** The idea that you cannot handle mental discomfort can be crippling. It can lead to rash or dangerous behaviors as a way of escaping mental discomfort.

• ***Lack of emotional control Skills:*** Without a toolbox of healthy coping strategies, managing overwhelming feelings becomes incredibly difficult. Individuals can fight to "shift" their mental state when needed.

• ***Invalidating Environments:*** Growing up in a setting that constantly ignores or invalidates your feelings can have a permanent effect. This can lead to confusion about your emotional experience and trouble believing your thoughts.

If these flaws aren't handled, people can fight to understand and control their feelings. Over time, bad coping strategies become habits, leading to constant trouble controlling feelings (chronic emotion dysregulation). This can cause problems like worry, sadness, and stress.

The effect of poor emotion efficiency and the fight to control feelings is vast, far-reaching, and also a common problem. Research shows that over 75% of people seeking psychotherapy deal with this very problem, regardless of their specific condition (Kring & Sloan, 2010). These persistent mental problems can significantly impact all areas of life, including relationships, work, and general well-being. In extreme cases, low emotion effectiveness can be life-interfering, leading to feelings of dread and sorrow.

Studies have shown a strong link between mood instability and a range of mental health issues. Higher levels of sadness, anxiety, recklessness, and even suicidal ideas have been linked to problems handling feelings successfully (Garnefski & Kraaij, 2007; Carver, Johnson, & Joormann, 2008; Kleiman & Riskind, 2012). Furthermore, mood instability can negatively impact the quality of life, memory, problem-solving skills, and general functioning (Richards & Gross, 2000; McCracken, Spertus, Janeck, Sinclair, & Wetzel, 1999; Marx & Sloan, 2002; Hayes, Luoma, Bond, Masuda, & Lillis, 2006). The ripple effects can stretch to social skills, drug abuse, and even a reduced sense of self-efficacy and feeling like you can't accomplish things (Berking et al., 2011; Eisenberg, Fabes, Guthrie, & Reiser, 2000; Caprara et al., 2008).

The good news is that emotional effectiveness can be better. Emotion Efficacy Therapy (EET) offers an organized and evidence-based method to help people build the skills and beliefs necessary to manage their emotional environment with greater skill and confidence. By addressing the underlying weaknesses and fostering healthy coping strategies, EET enables people to break free from the loop of low emotion effectiveness and build a more meaningful and emotionally healthy life.

Why Choose Emotion Efficacy Therapy (EET)? A Fresh Approach to Managing Your Emotions

Many people with Borderline Personality Disorder (BPD) deal with excessive emotions – worry, sadness, or just feeling out of control. They try different treatments, but often these treatments only focus on handling the symptoms, not the root cause of the problem. It's like taking medicine for a headache without finding out why you have headaches in the first place.

Here's why Emotion Efficacy Therapy (EET) offers a unique and possibly more successful and helpful method, especially for BPD:

Digging Deeper: Traditional methods might teach you coping skills, like breathing tactics. EET goes a step further. It helps you understand why controlling feelings is tough in the first place. This could be anything from having a natural tendency to feel emotions more strongly than others, to having grown up in a setting where your feelings weren't recognized. By solving these core reasons, EET aims for longer-lasting change.

Learning by Doing: Imagine learning to ride a bike just by reading a book. It wouldn't work very well, would it? EET stresses learning through practice. It's not just about learning skills; it's about practicing them in real-life scenarios so they become second nature. This "hands-on" method is important for BPD because it helps you apply these skills to your daily life. With EET, you'll gain confidence in handling tough feelings when they appear, a key factor in facing BPD difficulties.

Building Emotional Strength, Not Just Relief: Existing treatments can be helpful, but EET aims to be a more complete answer for BPD. It aims to provide a set of skills that you can use in any scenario, rather than just focusing on particular symptoms. Think of it like learning a new language – once you know the basics, you can speak in many different ways and handle the complexities of feelings with BPD. Once you know the basics of EET, you can build the mental strength needed to handle the strong feelings that are typical with BPD.

EET is built on the idea that some level of emotional pain is necessary in life. It's part of being human. However, pain doesn't have to be. Suffering often comes from two key things:

• ***Fighting the Flow:*** Many people with BPD try to push away tough feelings, which can actually make them worse. Trying to push away tough feelings can actually make them worse. Imagine trying to hold a beach ball underwater – the more you push, the harder it fights back. EET teaches you to accept these feelings as a normal part of life and to ride the emotional wave rather than getting swept away by it. This acceptance is important for people with BPD, who often deal with strong emotional reactions.

• ***Living Out of Alignment:*** Sometimes, pain comes from a gap between your deeds and your core ideals. For example, if you value honesty but keep lying to avoid conflict, you'll likely feel a sense of unease. EET helps you identify your values and guides you in reacting to tough feelings in a way that fits with those values, creating a more worthwhile and satisfying life. This focus on values-based action can be particularly helpful for people with BPD, who can deal with rash behaviors or trouble keeping good relationships.

EET gives you the skills to bridge the gap between feeling emotional triggers (events that set you off) and your natural responses. When you learn to handle this place carefully, you gain the power to choose answers that contribute to your well-being and fit with your values. The goal is to build a life where you feel real, powerful, and in control of your feelings. EET has the ability to improve the lives of millions dealing with emotional disorders. By improving your emotional effectiveness – the ability to handle a full range of feelings with acceptance, values-based action, and healthy coping – EET enables you to create a more real, powerful, and aware life. Imagine feeling comfortable with your emotions, knowing how to control them successfully, and living a life that shows who you truly are. That's the promise of Emotion Efficacy Therapy.

The Five Ingredients of Emotion Efficacy Therapy (EET)

Emotion Efficacy Therapy (EET) breaks down into five key parts that work together to help you control your feelings more successfully. Imagine these parts as building blocks – each one improves the next, leading to better mental well-being. Here's a better look at each of these five components:

1. Recognizing Your Emotions (Emotion Awareness)

Emotion Efficacy Therapy (EET) starts with a basic skill: noticing your feelings in the moment. This might seem simple, but it's often the first hurdle. We can get caught up in the daily grind, feeling emotions without truly knowing them. EET prepares you to become a keen watcher of your inner world.

EET goes beyond simply naming feelings as "happy" or "sad." It helps you recognize the minor differences within an emotion. For instance, you might be feeling slightly annoyed (like a small hassle) or extremely upset (a major obstacle) based on the situation. Recognizing these differences helps you to adjust coping strategies successfully. Emotions appear in different ways, not just through thoughts. EET underlines the value of identifying the:

Physical Sensations: A beating heart, sweaty hands, or a tight chest could indicate worry, while a flushed face, clenched jaw, and pounding fists could signal anger. By listening to these body cues, you gain important early signs of a rising mood.

Thoughts: Emotions often come with a music of thoughts. EET helps you recognize the thought processes associated with different feelings. Recognizing these trends allows you to question their truth and prevent them from feeding the emotional fire.

Urges to Act: Emotions can also appear as urges to act in certain ways. Feeling stressed might cause an urge to separate yourself, while anger might lead to the urge to act out orally. EET helps you spot these urges and teaches you to make a space between feeling and action. This break allows you to choose a more productive reaction.

By becoming an aware watcher of your feelings – their details, physical reactions, thought patterns, and related urges – you gain a better knowledge of yourself. This self-awareness is the basis upon which all other EET skills are built.

For Example:

Imagine you're waiting in a super long line at the store and you start to feel a little annoyed (like a drizzle). You might notice your shoulders getting tense and think, "This is slowing me down." EET teaches you healthy ways to deal with mild annoyance, like taking some deep breaths or listening to some calming music. Now, consider feeling super irritated (like rain) because you forgot an important talk at work. You might have a beating heart, sweaty hands, and a bunch of thoughts like, "I can't believe I did this again!" EET gives you tools to handle this stronger emotional state, such as practicing mindfulness techniques or telling yourself to be kind to yourself (because everyone makes mistakes!).

Through Emotion Awareness, EET helps you become a weather forecaster for your own feelings. By recognizing the early signs of an emotional storm, you can take steps to handle it before it gets too out of control. This opens the way for the next step of EET: Mindful Acceptance, where you learn to accept your feelings, not fight them.

2. Accepting Your Emotions (Mindful Acceptance)

Think about your day-to-day life. You're running out the door, late for work, and your stomach twists with worry. Maybe you're stuck in traffic and anger starts to bubble up, showing as a locked jaw and a string of whispered words under your breath. These are your emotional waves, and Mindful Acceptance in EET shows you how to handle them in real-time. Mindful Acceptance isn't about forcing a smile or acting like everything is sunshine and flowers. It's recognizing and accepting all your feelings, the good, the bad, and the ugly, without judgment. It's like opening a haven within yourself where all your feelings can be present – the nervous spark of excitement before a first date and the heavy weight of sadness after a job rejection. Here are some steps to adopt Mindful Acceptance in the heat of the moment:

Check-In with Your Body: Take a physical inventory. Is your heart racing? Are your arms tense? Notice these body feelings without judgment. They're simply signs that something intense is brewing.

Name the Emotion Without Judgment: Once you know the physical signs, name the emotion. Are you feeling nervous, angry, or overwhelmed? Simply label the emotion – "I'm feeling anxious" or "There's frustration here." Avoid naming yourself ("I'm such a worrier") or adding bad meanings to the emotion ("This frustration is ruining everything").

Challenge Negative Thoughts: Emotions often come with harmful thinking habits. When you recognize the feeling, pay attention to the thoughts connected with it. Are you catastrophizing? For example, with job worry, are you thinking "I'm going to mess up everything and get fired"? Challenge these negative thoughts with more realistic and powerful ones. Maybe it's, "I'm prepared, and I can handle whatever comes up."

Engage Your Senses: Sometimes centering yourself in the present moment can help interrupt the emotional wave. Focus on your feelings. What do you see? Hear? Smell? Take a few deep breaths and feel the coolness of the air entering your lungs. This simple act can bring your attention back to the present and lessen the strength of the feeling.

Real-Life Examples

Example 1: The Work Presentation

You're giving a talk, and your hands start to sweat, and your heart starts to race. (Check-In with Your Body) You recognize this as worry. (Name the Emotion) Instead of letting negative thoughts grow ("I'm going to bomb!"), question them with statements ("I'm prepared," "I've practiced this"). (Challenge Negative Thoughts) Finally, take a few deep breaths and focus on the sound of your voice as you begin to talk. (Engage Your Senses)

Example 2: The Traffic Jam

You're stuck in bumper-to-bumper traffic, and anger starts to simmer. (Check In With Your Body) You know the feeling and name it anger. (Name the Emotion) Instead of letting the frustration boil over and lead to road rage, challenge the thought, "This is going to ruin my whole day," with a more realistic one, "There's nothing I can do about the traffic, but I can control how I react." (Challenge Negative Thoughts) Finally, put on some calming music and focus on your breathing. (Engage Your Senses)

Example 3: The Disagreement

You're having an argument with a friend, and anger starts to rise. (Check-In with Your Body) You know the feeling of anger. (Name the Emotion) Notice the thought, "They're being so unreasonable!" Challenge this by telling yourself of your friend's good traits. (Challenge Negative Thoughts) Take a time out from the talk and engage your senses by focusing on something calming in the surroundings, like a gentle breeze or a colorful flower. (Engage Your Senses)

With Mindful Acceptance and Emotion Awareness as your basis, EET enables you to take the next step: Values-Based Action. Here, you'll learn to put your core values into real acts, even in the face of difficult feelings. This allows you to not only understand and accept your feelings but also to harness them as a guide, leading you towards a life that reflects your true self.

3. Aligning Your Actions with Your Values (Values-Based Action)

VBA comes into play after you've built the base of emotional awareness and mindful acceptance. Now you can spot those times of choice – the space between feeling an emotion (jealousy) and responding to it (lashing out). This is your chance to choose an answer that fits with your core values, not just your passing feelings.

The first step in VBA is finding out what truly matters to you. EET helps you discover your core ideals in different parts of your life:

• **Work:** Integrity, speed, collaboration?

• **Home:** Honesty, love, supportiveness?

• **Relationships:** Honesty, respect, affection?

• **Personal Growth:** Learning, challenge, self-improvement?

• **Community:** Social justice, environmental duty, helping others?

By finding your ideals in each area, you gain an understanding of what's truly important to you. Once you know your beliefs, EET helps you put them into specific activities. For example, if you value honesty at work but are feeling nervous about standing up in a meeting, VBA prepares you to do so. You might choose to practice what you want to say beforehand or imagine yourself sharing your opinion quietly and firmly.

Example 1: Jealousy at Work

Value: Fairness

Emotion: Jealousy (of colleague's rise)

VBA: Schedule a meeting with your boss to talk about job growth possibilities. This allows you to show your desire (another possible value) effectively, matching with fairness and possibly improving your mental state in the long run.

Example 2: Anger at Home

Value: Respectful Communication

Emotion: Anger (at your partner for leaving food dirty)

VBA: Take a deep breath and use "I" words to describe your anger. For example, "I feel disrespected when the dishes are left unwashed because we agreed to share chores." This method supports open communication and addresses the problem directly, matching with polite communication and possibly lowering total anger. Just like any skill, VBA takes practice to learn. EET uses exposure-based skills training to help you practice picking values-based actions in safe, controlled settings.

Here are two ways EET helps you learn VBA:

Emotion Exposure: You might remember a past case where you didn't act in line with your values due to a strong emotion. Then, you'd practice how you could have reacted differently using VBA. Imagine being jealous of your colleague's rise again. You could practice how to thank them truly, matching with a possible value of supportiveness.

Imaginal Exposure: Imagine a future situation that might spark a tough feeling. Then, imagine yourself using VBA to choose an answer that fits with your values. For example, picture coming home to find dirty dishes again. Visualize yourself using "I" words to express your anger quietly, matching with respectful communication.

By frequently practicing VBA in engaged states (feeling the feelings), you build the confidence and ability to use it successfully in real-life situations, eventually improving your emotional effectiveness.

The Benefits of VBA And Why VBA is Essential for EET

VBA is about more than just feeling good in the moment. Research shows that having a life that fits with your beliefs is linked to better psychological well-being and a higher quality of life (Hayes, Strosahl, & Wilson, 1999; Ruiz, 2010). EET goes beyond simply managing feelings. It aims to enable you to build a useful and satisfying life, thereby improving your emotional effectiveness. VBA is a core EET skill because:

Increased Motivation: Knowing you're acting on your ideals makes it easier to commit to new and possibly tough habits, like having a hard talk at work.

Reduced Distress: By picking values-based actions, you break the loop of responding quickly to feelings (like breaking out in anger), which can eventually reduce general distress.

Improved Emotional Regulation: Over time, regularly acting on your values can lead to a better knowledge of your emotional causes and how to control them successfully.

Improved Quality of Life: Living a life that fits with your values creates a sense of sincerity and purpose, leading to a richer and more worthwhile life, eventually adding to greater emotional effectiveness.

In sum, VBA is the bridge between emotional awareness and motivated action. By choosing to react based on your values, you take control of your mental experience and build a life that truly reflects who you are. This, in turn, promotes a sense of emotional control – a key component of emotional effectiveness.

Identify Your Emotional Triggers. What events or people tend to trigger strong feelings in you? Once you know your triggers, you can predict them and plan a values-based reaction.

Be Flexible: Your values can vary slightly based on the situation. For example, at work, speed might be a core value, while at home, spending valuable time with family might take precedence. VBA pushes you to be flexible and choose the value most important to the case.

Self-compassion is Key: Don't beat yourself up if you don't always react exactly according to your ideals. VBA is a skill that takes time and practice to learn. Be kind to yourself as you learn and grow.

By adding VBA into your daily life, you can move beyond simply handling feelings and start living a life led by your core values. This method enables you to handle tough situations with greater emotional resilience and creates a sense of emotional well-being – the sign of successful emotional effectiveness.

4. Healthy Coping Skills in a Crisis (Mindful Coping)

The emotional impact of a disaster can sometimes make careful acceptance feel like an impossible task. This is where conscious living comes in. It's a crucial idea in EET, especially meant to address situations where emotional overload makes mindful acceptance difficult. Here's what makes thoughtful dealing unique:

1. Mindful Acceptance as the Gateway: Unlike traditional coping methods that focus solely on ignoring or dodging feelings, mindful coping starts with mindful acceptance. This means noting the feeling without judgment and noticing its physical sensations and related thoughts. Even during a crisis, taking a moment to recognize the emotional storm building within you provides a vital place for choosing a healthy coping skill.

2. Noticing the Moment of Choice: Mindful coping hinges on noticing a key moment – the moment of choice. This is the place between having an intense emotion and responding quickly to it. In the hurricane comparison, it's the moment you understand you need to take cover, before the storm's full force hits.

3. Choosing Wisely: Coping as a Tool, not a Crutch: Once you notice the moment of choice, mindful coping urges you to choose a coping skill, but with a specific purpose. It's not about pushing the feeling away or silencing yourself. Instead, the goal is to downregulate the feeling, bringing its strength to a reasonable level. This helps you to recover some mental control and make clear, values-based choices.

Think of it this way: Imagine the storm has ripped off part of your roof. You might need to patch it up briefly with a tarp (coping skill) to avoid further damage until the storm passes. Then, you can focus on the more lasting fixes (mindful acceptance and values-based action).

Mindful Coping Skills in Action

EET offers a variety of mindful coping skills that you can use to downregulate strong emotions:

• ***Deep Breathing:*** Taking slow, deep breaths triggers your body's relaxation response, counteracting the physical effects of strong feelings like worry.

• ***Progressive Muscle Relaxation:*** Tensing and releasing different muscle groups can help release built-up tension linked with mental discomfort.

• ***Mindfulness Meditation:*** Focusing your attention on the current moment and watching your thoughts and feelings without judgment can create a sense of calm amidst the storm.

• ***Visualization:*** Imagine yourself in a safe and calming place to produce a feeling of peace and lessen emotional energy.

• ***Engaging Your Senses:*** Focus on your senses – what do you see, hear, smell, or taste? Grounding yourself in the present moment through your senses can help interrupt the emotional storm.

You learn to not only handle regular emotional waves but also to control strong feelings successfully. This sets the stage for the next part of EET, Values-Based Action, where you'll study how to put your core values into specific actions, even in the face of difficult feelings. This ensures that you not only survive the storms but also use them as a chance for growth and self-discovery. The thoughtful coping skills you learn become a bridge, helping you move from stress to a place where you can choose actions that reflect your real values.

5. Putting It All Together: Practicing in Real Life (Exposure-Based Skills Practice)

Exposure-based skills practice is a cornerstone of Emotion Efficacy Therapy (EET), a powerful method for growing emotional resiliency. It's not about idly learning coping strategies; it's about actively interacting with your feelings in a safe and controlled setting to improve your ability to handle them successfully.

This exercise uses two key techniques:

Emotion Exposure:

Imagine yourself facing a situation that usually triggers worry or anger. In exposure-based skills practice, you'd consciously remember this scene and purposefully trigger those feelings within yourself – but in a safe, therapy setting led by a therapist.

This action helps you to practice the EET skills you've learned, such as mindful acceptance and mindful living.

Real-life Example: Let's say you have a fear of public speech. During exposure-based practice, you might share a past talk that caused nervousness. You'd then intentionally relive those nervous feelings while practicing conscious acceptance – acknowledging the physical sensations and thoughts connected with anxiety without judgment.

Imaginal Exposure (Imagery-Based Exposure):

This method involves using detailed images to create an accurate representation of a possible future situation that causes emotional discomfort. For instance, if you deal with social nervousness, you might imagine yourself going to a party. As the picture evokes anxiety, you'd practice applying your EET skills, such as picturing yourself using deep breathing exercises or engaging in positive self-talk to control your anxiety successfully.

Real-life Example: Imagine you have a job interview coming up that makes you feel stressed. In imaginal exposure, you'd work with your therapist to build a clear mental image of the interview setting, imagining yourself feeling nervous. You'd then practice picturing yourself utilizing coping strategies like relaxing methods or positive mantras to maintain emotional calm during the actual interview.

The success of exposure-based practice lies in its ability to:

Enhance Learning and Retention: Actively training your EET skills while feeling heightened emotions increases the brain paths linked with those skills. This makes it more likely you'll be able to reach and utilize them effectively in real-world conditions.

Improve Recall: Recalling past events and feelings during exposure practice improves the memory of the skills you've learned. You're basically building a "mental muscle memory" that you can easily trigger when faced with similar problems in the future.

Facilitate Effective Choices: By practicing EET skills during imagined emotional activation, you become more adept at making value-based choices even when feeling pain. You learn to choose healthy coping methods instead of being swept away by negative feelings.

Think of exposure-based skills practice as a mental gym. Just like physical training improves your body, this method increases your mental toughness. By carefully dealing with your feelings in a controlled setting, you develop the tools and confidence to handle difficult scenarios with greater calmness and control. Imagine trying to learn how to ride a bike just by reading a book. It wouldn't work very well, would it? EET emphasizes the importance of practicing your skills in real-life scenarios. By constantly training your skills in engaged states, you build the confidence and ability to use them successfully when you face difficult situations in your daily life.

Overall, these five components of EET work together to allow you to take charge of your emotional experience. By building your emotional awareness, practicing acceptance, matching your actions with your values, using healthy coping skills, and putting it all into practice, EET allows you to create a life filled with better emotional well-being and a sense of living truly.

Interpersonal Effectiveness

Healthy relationships are the basis of a happy life. But for those dealing with emotional control, managing the complexities of human relationships can be a minefield. This is especially true for people with Borderline Personality Disorder (BPD). Here's where Dialectical Behavior Therapy (DBT) steps in, giving a toolkit for handling the dance of relationships with greater ease.

Our feelings are deeply linked with the quality of our interactions. This is particularly true for those who have trouble controlling their feelings. When relationships are safe and loving, they provide a sense of security, working as a protection against mental turbulence. Conversely, insecure or unhealthy relationships can exacerbate mental turmoil, often leading to self-destructive behaviors that further complicate things. Additionally, the lack of strong relationships can leave individuals feeling isolated and sad.

Humans are social beings, and strong social ties are important for well-being. Therefore, taking stock of your support system is important. Do you have a network of friends and acquaintances? Who in your family are you close to? Are there faith communities or social groups you join that offer a sense of belonging and support? Even online bonds, while missing actual contact, can be a source of closeness for some. The key feature to consider isn't simply the amount of contacts you have, but the strength of those links. Do they bring joy and satisfaction? Or are they a cause of negativity and conflict? It's important to be honest with yourself about these relationships.

It's normal to have different wants when it comes to partnerships. Some people are introverts, happy with a smaller group, while others crave a larger social network. There's no right or wrong – the goal is to feel satisfied by the relationships you have. Once you've assessed your social life, ask yourself: "Am I happy with this? Do my relationships leave me feeling supported and complete?" Don't ignore challenges like social anxiety that might hinder your ability to correctly assess your needs.

You can sometimes disagree with someone's evaluation of their relationships. You could think they should make new friends or cut ties with those they don't feel good about. Recall that every person has distinct demands. It's more crucial to pay attention to how satisfied they are with their present network. DBT can support an individual in exploring choices if they recognize that they don't have satisfying relationships and that they would want to have more social interaction. This might be repairing and strengthening current relationships, fostering closer bonds with people they already know, or going out and forming whole new relationships.

Communication Styles: Understanding How We Talk (and Don't Talk)

In every relationship, communication is essential. It's how we establish a connection, communicate our emotions, and work through life's challenges together. However, communication styles differ from one another, much like individuals, and they don't all match well. We'll look at four typical communication philosophies here and how they affect our relationships.

Indeed, let us include BPD in the communication styles segment to get a more all-encompassing image:

How We Talk (and Don't Talk) - Particularly for People with BPD

In every relationship, communication is essential. However, negotiating the nuances of communication styles can be far more difficult for those who are dealing with Borderline Personality Disorder (BPD). Having trouble expressing oneself efficiently and clearly can be caused by a variety of factors, including intense emotions, a fear of being abandoned, and black-and-white thinking. Four typical communication styles will be discussed here, along with how they can affect our relationships and how they could show up in a person with BPD.

The Silent Treatment: Passive Communication

It is common for passive communicators to go unnoticed. They can suppress their feelings because they don't think their needs are significant or because they dread conflict. A person with BPD can find it difficult to appropriately communicate their strong feelings, which makes this silence more noticeable. Imagine having a BPD person who constantly consents to plans they don't like, never expresses their thoughts, and keeps their demands to themselves. While this passive strategy could maintain calm in the short term, if their demands are not addressed over time, anger can grow. Additionally, the unclear message can cause the person receiving it to feel uneasy or puzzled.

Example:

- Consistently accepting proposals that you find objectionable without bringing them up.
- Letting problems fester instead of having tough talks.
- Muttered "fine" when being upset.

Think about this: How often do you use passive communication? Did it provide the intended results?

Who do you usually apply this style to?

What effects, if any, do you believe this relationship style has on people, particularly those who have BPD?

Aggressive Communication: The Verbal Juggernaut

Aggressive communication is at the opposite extreme of the spectrum. These talkers often control discussions by talking over and interrupting others. To make their point, they could be critical, sarcastic, or even threatening. This violent style can be triggered in a person with BPD by great anger or a sense of invalidation. Imagine a person with borderline personality disorder (BPD) who belittles you, speaks down to you, and places blame to get their way. Although at first glance this tactic can appear aggressive, it often provokes defensiveness and ends fruitful conversations, driving loved ones away—a worry that is frequently at the heart of borderline personality disorder.

As an example:

- Making a point by using insults or sarcasm.
- Monopolizing talks and interjecting as necessary.
- Using threats or demands as a means of achieving your goals.

Think: What instances of forceful communication have you used? Did it result in anything good?

Who do you usually apply this style to?

What effects, if any, do you believe this relationship style has on people, particularly those who have BPD?

The Unspoken Word: Aggressive/Passive Communication

It might be challenging to negotiate passive-aggressive communication. Although the outward appearance of these communicators can be pleasing, their actions or behaviors suggest otherwise. They can give the silent treatment, make snide remarks, or consistently arrive late. Let's say you have a BPD person who agrees to assist you with a project, but they often miss deadlines or provide poor-quality work. This manipulative strategy can originate from a fear of closeness or an unconscious attempt to drive someone away before abandoning them. It leads to misunderstandings and dissatisfaction, eventually hindering development and undermining interpersonal trust.

Examples:

- Agreeing to something but then finding excuses not to do it.
- Giving backhanded compliments or making sarcastic remarks.
- Using the silent treatment to express anger or disapproval.

Think about this: When did you use passive-aggressive communication? Did it provide the intended results?

Who do you usually apply this style to?

What effects, if any, do you believe this relationship style has on people, particularly those who have BPD?

The Art of Assertiveness: Discovering Your Voice, Particularly in the Case of BPD

A balance between the extremes is achieved via assertive communication. While simultaneously honoring the rights of others, assertive communicators are straightforward and honest in expressing their needs, wishes, and views. They take responsibility for their emotions and steer clear of accusing language by using "I" expressions. Imagine a person with BPD who discusses their problems in a calm and nonjudgmental manner, actively listens to the other person and looks for solutions that benefit both sides. For those with

BPD who want connection and worry about being abandoned, assertiveness builds connections and promotes mutual respect and understanding.

Examples: "I get annoyed when last-minute changes are made to my plans. "Can we talk about how we can improve our communication going forward?"

"Thank you for your assistance, but I'd rather do this myself. I'm not comfortable with that choice. Are there any other possibilities we might look into?"

Think about this: When did you use aggressive communication? Did it result in anything good?

Who do you usually apply this style to?

*What effects, if any, do you believe this relationship style has on people, particularly those who have BPD?

For someone with BPD, learning how to communicate assertively can be very powerful. They can use it to strengthen and protect their relationships, advocate for themselves, and healthily express their feelings. People with BPD can lessen their fear of being abandoned and develop trust with loved ones by developing assertive communication skills.

Further suggestions for enhancing communication, particularly for those with BPD, are as follows:

Verify Your Feelings: Before you communicate your sentiments to other people, acknowledge your own. A more composed dialogue is made possible by this self-awareness, which also helps prevent emotional outbursts.

Make use of "I" statements: Use statements like "I feel" or "I need" rather than critical ones to take responsibility for your emotions. This facilitates constructive communication and defuses tense situations.

Active listening: entails paying great attention to both spoken and unspoken communication from the other person. Review what you've heard to make sure you understand and to make sure there are no misconceptions.

Define Boundaries: It's critical to set up sound limits in partnerships. Express your expectations and demands in a kind and straightforward manner.

Seek Assistance: To manage BPD symptoms and improve communication skills, think about attending counseling or support groups.

Recall that effective communication is an acquired talent. Celebrate your accomplishments and exercise self-compassion. You can forge deeper, more satisfying connections and confidently negotiate the intricacies of BPD by deliberately selecting aggressive communication.

HOW TO MASTER ASSERTIVENESS

1. Set Priorities for Your Goals: The Foundation of Assertive Communication

To communicate effectively, you must be aware of your true desires. Take a deliberate moment to determine your primary goal in the circumstance before you engage in any discussion. The following are some possible priorities that you can run into:

Goal Attainment: Do you ask the other person to assist you in reaching a certain objective? Maybe you need their support on an idea or assistance with a project.

Connection Building: Is fostering and fortifying the connection itself your main goal? Perhaps you want to show gratitude or just establish a stronger connection.

Self-Assured Expression: Irrespective of the result, do you just like to feel self-assured and secure in your ability to express yourself? This might include establishing limits or voicing disagreeing views.

Saying No: If a request doesn't fit your requirements or timetable, you may need to gently deny it.

It might be challenging at times to balance many objectives. While it can be ideal to do all of them at once, setting priorities is occasionally necessary. Having unwavering clarity on your main objective is essential, regardless of the result you want to achieve. Just picture attempting to strike a target that you are not sure where it is! You can then decide which communication skills will help you get closer to your main goal after you've determined what it is.

2. Assertive Requests: How to Maintain Harmony While Getting What You Need

Gaining the ability to communicate assertively will enable you to politely, directly, and clearly state your demands and objectives. However, identifying your goals is only half the fight. Making requests that accomplish your goals without endangering the relationship is the real art. Here's a summary of the crucial actions to take:

Step 1: Establishing the Groundwork - An Objective Account

Setting the stage for your request is the next step after determining your top priority, as was previously described. Start by clearly and impartially outlining the circumstances. Don't use judgmental or accusing language; just stick to the facts. Recall that the intention here is to simply portray the situation as a problem in need of a solution, not to place blame or instigate conflict.

Consider the following situation: Your colleague often misses deadlines on important assignments, which means you are always running late.

A nonjudgmental explanation would go something like this: "Recently, there have been a few times when deadlines haven't been met on projects we collaborate on, which has caused some delays on my end." Rather than accusing someone of being always late and disrupting things.

Step 2: Owning Your Experience by Putting Your Thoughts and Feelings Into Expression

The next action is to openly express your emotions and ideas regarding the circumstance. Inform the other person of the effect their actions are having on you. Taking responsibility for your feelings encourages empathy and makes room for sincere conversation.

Using the colleague as an example once again, let's say that missing deadlines increases the pressure on you to do your job on time.

Here, you're communicating how their behaviors affect you without using derogatory words.

Step 3: The Art of the Ask: Putting Forward a Polite and Stated Request

NOW is the time to be assertive! This is the time to express your intended result in unambiguous terms. What does the individual need or desire from you? Make a request that is both courteous and detailed.

You might wrap up your discussion with the colleague like this: "Maybe we could set up a system where we check in on deadlines a little early to prevent similar delays in the future. Perhaps sending out weekly progress updates might keep us on course."

These guidelines can help you ask for what you need authoritatively and courteously while still keeping a good rapport with the other person. Recall that effective communication involves both parties. Investigate ideas that benefit you both and be receptive to hearing their point of view. Practice makes perfect when it comes to assertiveness. If you don't get it flawless every time, don't give up. Appreciate your accomplishments; with persistent work, you'll be able to move gracefully and confidently through the dance of aggressive demands.

3. The Art of Win-Win: Assertive Communication Through Negotiation

Good communication is a collaborative dance rather than a monologue. Aggressive communication gives you the capacity to effectively communicate your requirements, but it also understands how important it is to respect other people's viewpoints. Finding common ground via negotiation is essential to reaching mutually beneficial agreements.

Recognizing the Influence of "Give and Take"

Consider the following situation: As previously said, you've gently but firmly communicated to your buddy that their frequent last-minute changes to plans cause you to be late. It doesn't end there for a forceful strategy. It recognizes that your buddy can have demands and preferences of their own.

Through negotiation, you can look at options that benefit both of you. To make sure you're both on schedule, maybe you might decide on a deadline for finishing plans. Perhaps you might set up several alternatives for activities, some planned and others impromptu, to accommodate your tastes.

Advantages of Teamwork in Solutions

There are several advantages to looking for solutions that all parties can accept:

Enhanced Cooperation: When both sides believe their demands are being taken into account, they are more inclined to work together to develop solutions.

Improved Bonds: By concentrating on win-win solutions, you can build mutual respect and understanding, which can ultimately deepen your connection.

Innovation in Solving Problems: Creative problem-solving that could not have been thought of otherwise can be sparked by negotiation.

Changing the Subject: From "Me" to "We"

A change in viewpoint is encouraged by assertive communication, as opposed to concentrating just on meeting your wants. The goal is to arrive at a solution that benefits all parties involved. Here are some pointers to help you do this:

Engaging in Active Listening: Keep a tight eye on what the other person says, both with words and body language. In addition to showing respect, this aids in determining their true requirements and worries.

Brainstorming Ideas: Collaborate to produce an array of possible answers. Keep an open mind and consider all of your alternatives.

Locating Common Ground: Start by identifying points of agreement and expanding on them. Establish common objectives and work together to achieve them.

Recall that effective negotiation requires practice. When attempting to discover common ground, use patience with both the other person and yourself. Assertive communication can help you create win-win situations and better connections by focusing on mutual gain and being ready to compromise. Being assertive does not entail always achieving what you want. Compromise is sometimes required. But, it's crucial to stay away from circumstances in which you continuously put the wants of the other person above your own. Through negotiation, you can reach a mutually beneficial agreement in which both sides feel appreciated and respected.

4. Acknowledging the Opposite Viewpoint: An Essential Measure in Bold Communicating with BPD

It might be difficult for people with Borderline Personality Disorder (BPD) to communicate. Complicated emotions, despondency, and binary thinking can make it difficult to see things from other people's viewpoints. But developing your ability to gather information—that is, actively trying to ascertain the needs, goals, ideas, and emotions of the other person—will help you manage BPD symptoms and forge closer bonds with your partner.

The Significance of Understanding

Imagine if a friend of yours with BPD often cancels arrangements at the last minute, leaving you feeling betrayed and confused. Being assertive involves more than just voicing your annoyance. It goes deeper, trying to figure out why your buddy acts in this manner. Maybe their busy job schedule causes them to forget, or maybe they have social anxiety that makes them uneasy in big gatherings. You can get important insights that will enable you to handle the issue with more understanding and empathy by actively searching out information.

The Advantages of Information Seeking

When people with BPD actively seek knowledge during conversation, there are several advantages:

Diminished Emotional Reactivity: It's simpler to control your own emotions when you know the "why" behind someone's behavior. This can promote more composed conversation and help avoid rash decisions.

Enhanced Trust: Taking the effort to comprehend another person's viewpoint demonstrates your appreciation for their emotions. In the long term, this enhances the connection by fostering trust.

Developing Original Solutions: You can come up with ideas for solutions that benefit both of you if you are aware of the demands of the other person. If your buddy has social anxiety, maybe you might agree on more manageable and consistent meetups.

Active Listening: The Understanding Bridge

Asking questions is not the only way to get information. It entails active listening, which is paying great attention to the other person's verbal and nonverbal clues. The following active listening advice is very beneficial for people with BPD:

Be in the moment: Make eye contact and put aside any distractions to demonstrate your attention. This will enable you to control your emotions and concentrate on the discussion.

Confirm Their Emotions: Be mindful of their feelings, even if you disagree with them. This shows empathy and establishes a secure environment for candid dialogue.

Pose Explicit Questions: Emotions can sometimes impede communication. To make sure you fully grasp their viewpoint, use open-ended questions.

An Example Situation: Engaging in Active Listening with BPD

Using the example from before as a guide, the following is how you can use active listening to comprehend your friend's viewpoint:

You: "When plans change at the last minute, it hurts and confuses me. Could you elaborate on what's happening for you at that point?

You can get important information that will enable you to handle the circumstance with more compassion and understanding by asking an open-ended inquiry and paying close attention to the answer.

Creating Connectional Bridges

For people with BPD in particular, the foundation of assertive communication is attempting to understand the other person. This comprehension facilitates empathy, lessens emotional reactions, and opens the door to discovering points of agreement. You can create more satisfying relationships and better manage the symptoms of BPD by adding information-seeking and active listening to your communication toolkit. Recall that information acquisition requires reciprocity. Be willing to share your ideas and emotions as well. This reciprocity fortifies the bond and promotes trust.

5. The Art of Saying No: Safeguarding Your Relationships and Yourself with BPD

It might be very difficult for those with Borderline Personality Disorder (BPD) to say no. Black-and-white thinking and a deep fear of abandonment might make it seem as if a rejection would terminate the relationship completely. On the other hand, you can say no and yet defend your needs and relationships when you communicate assertively.

Recognizing the Significance of Limitations

Consider the following situation: You believe that your social obligations are too much for someone with BPD. When a buddy invites you to a big party, you're delighted at first, but the idea of being in a busy, stimulating place wears you out soon. Establishing sound limits and politely expressing your wants and limitations are key components of an aggressive strategy. Refusing the party enables you to put your health first and prevent emotional exhaustion. Long-term, this enhances the relationship since you will be more positive and balanced when you do spend time together.

Advantages of Having an Assertive No

When people with BPD exercise assertive rejection, they get several benefits:

Diminished Emotional Anguish: By establishing limits and refusing requests when necessary, you save yourself from being overburdened and emotionally spent. This enables you to better control the symptoms of your BPD.

Better Regard for Oneself: Saying no and putting your needs first show respect for yourself. This promotes a positive connection with oneself and increases your feeling of self-worth.

Stronger (Paradoxical!) Relationships: Contrary to popular belief, relationships can be strengthened by having the courage to say no when necessary. In the long term, you're better able to be a present and helpful friend if you respect your own needs.

Saying No with Respect and Empathy

The main point is "no," but how you say it counts. Here are some pointers for politely declining requests without compromising your relationship:

Accept the Request: Recognize the other person's words by nodding in quick response to their request.

Say "Thank You": I appreciate their considering you and involving you.

Justify Your Decision (Optional): Give a brief explanation of your inability to attend, being careful not to include extraneous information or arguments. Saying anything like "I have a prior commitment that evening" or "I'm feeling a bit overwhelmed lately" would suffice.

Provide an Optional Alternate: If suitable, recommend another method of communication. Perhaps you might suggest a more intimate meeting or a private coffee date soon.

Example Situation: Refusing with BPD

Building on the last example, the following describes how you can turn down the invitation to the party by using forceful communication:

You: "I really appreciate you inviting me to the celebration! Such sounds like a great time. To be honest, I've been feeling a little overwhelmed recently and I don't think I could have a great time in such a large crowd. Perhaps we could meet up over coffee sometime next week?"

This method accepts the invitation, shows gratitude, and provides a succinct answer without giving away too much. Additionally, it offers another avenue for communication, indicating your want to keep the connection going. Recall that refusing is a right, not an honor. When used assertively, it preserves your health and improves your connections with others. You can become an expert at saying no and create relationships that are better and more rewarding with practice and self-compassion.

6. Living with Integrity: Linking Your Behavior to Your Principles for Better BPD Relationships

Borderline Personality Disorder (BPD) can sometimes result in problems with decision-making and self-worth. On the other hand, acting in line with your beliefs and values via bold speech gives you the ability to live a worthy life. This builds equal respect and trust in your relationships in addition to improving your sense of self.

The Power of Alignment

Imagine this scenario: You (with BPD) are pushed by a friend to join them in sharing gossip about a close acquaintance. You know this goes against your core values of honesty and kindness. An assertive strategy includes matching your behaviors with your beliefs. This means saying no to your friend, even though the fear of loss might make it tempting to cave in.

Living with ethics allows you to make choices you can be proud of. It promotes self-respect and a strong sense of self-worth, which are crucial for handling BPD conditions.

Benefits of Living with Integrity

There are numerous perks for those with BPD when they practice life with integrity:

Increased Self-Esteem: When your deeds match with your beliefs, your sense of self-worth gets a boost. This inner strength turns into more confident conversations and better interactions.

Reduced Emotional Distress: Aligning your behavior with your morals lowers internal strife and creates a feeling of peace. This, in turn, helps handle emotional instability, a common sign of BPD.

Stronger Relationships: People are pulled to those who are real and trustworthy. Living with ethics creates trust and respect in your relationships, creating a more helpful atmosphere.

Honesty and Assertiveness: A Powerful Combination

While honesty is key, it's important to give it assertively to avoid causing pointless tension or hurting relationships. Here are some tips for speaking honestly and assertively:

"I" Statements: Use "I" sentences to describe your beliefs and why you can't join in the action. For example, "I feel uncomfortable talking about others. It goes against my values of honesty."

Focus on Your Feelings: Explain how the situation makes you feel, rather than attacking the other person's character. This promotes understanding and lowers defensiveness.

Offer Alternatives: If suitable, offer different ways to spend time with your friend that fit with your values.

Sample Scenario: Aligning Actions with Values

Following up on the previous example, here's how you might use strong speech to reject your friend's request:

You: "I appreciate you asking me to trust in you, but I'm not comfortable talking about [acquaintance's name]. Honestly, it makes me feel nervous. How about we watch a movie instead?"

This method clearly expresses your opinion without judgment. It also offers a different exercise, showing your desire to keep the bond.

Finding the Balance: White Lies and Self-Respect

The part recognizes the rare need for white lies in social settings. While full honesty is best, there are times when a careful white lie can maintain a connection. The key is to use judgment and avoid depending on them too frequently.

Living with ethics doesn't mean being completely honest all the time. It's about finding a balance between honesty and respect. By matching your actions with your beliefs and speaking assertively, you can build better, more important relationships and handle BPD symptoms more effectively.

Beyond the Basics: Mastering Assertive Communication for Stronger Relationships with BPD

While the core principles of forceful communication are basic, additional methods can further encourage those with BPD to handle difficult scenarios and build better connections. Here are some useful tools to add to your conversation toolbox:

Deepening Your Understanding: Mindful Listening

Active, not passive: Mindful listening goes beyond simply being quiet while the other person talks. It includes giving close attention to both verbal and unconscious cues, like body language and tone of voice. This shows respect and helps you gain a better understanding of their viewpoint.

Benefits: When you truly listen, the other person feels heard and respected. This promotes trust and provides a safe place for open conversation. Additionally, careful listening allows you to spot possible areas of agreement or balance, leading to more productive encounters.

Acknowledge, not condone: Validation doesn't mean agreeing with someone's deeds; it means accepting their feelings and experiences. For example, "I understand you're feeling frustrated" supports someone's anger without actually approving their behavior.

Benefits of Validation: Validation shows understanding and provides a feeling of closeness. It often de-escalates anger and helps the talk to move forward more helpfully. This is particularly helpful for those with BPD who can deal with emotional instability.

Beyond black and white: BPD can lead to black-and-white thinking, making it difficult to see multiple views. Dialectical thinking pushes you to consider both sides of a problem and understand that seemingly opposing opinions can coexist.

Benefits: Dialectical thinking promotes understanding and reduces the chance of getting stuck in power battles. It allows you to find common ground and approach problems with more freedom, leading to answers that work for everyone.

Willingness, not weakness: Adopting an open approach in conversation shows your desire to consider different views and work towards a solution. It doesn't suggest weakness or a lack of resolve.

Benefits: Openness creates trust and cooperation. It also allows you to add fun and lightheartedness to the talk, creating a more upbeat and relaxed environment.

Authenticity over appeasement: Excessive explanations can weaken your self-respect and erode self-esteem. Only apologize when truly deserved – when you've made a mistake or caused someone hurt.

Owning Your Actions: When an apology is due, take full blame and show real sorrow. This shows growth and improves trust in the partnership.

These methods are not meant to be a hard plan, but rather a fluid toolbox to draw from as required. With constant practice and self-compassion, you can learn forceful speech and build better, more satisfying relationships, successfully handling BPD symptoms along the way.

A major difference between DBT and CBT lies in their method of change. CBT often focuses on finding and changing skewed thought habits. While DBT recognizes the role of harmful thinking habits, it puts strong stress on accepting yourself as you are in the present moment. This self-acceptance promotes a sense of self-compassion, building a basis for positive change. Validation is another cornerstone of DBT. Your therapist actively listens to you without judgment and accepts the truth of your feelings and experiences. This provides a safe place where you feel heard and understood, promoting trust and teamwork. The therapy connection holds great importance in DBT. Unlike the more distant method sometimes seen in CBT, DBT therapists try to build a real relationship with you. This strong union becomes a powerful tool for helping you on your journey. Here's how the therapy connection promotes healing in DBT:

Validation: As mentioned earlier, therapists actively listen without judgment and support your feelings and experiences. This promotes a sense of trust and helps you to feel safe discovering your weaknesses.

Modeling Healthy Relationships: Through their relationships with you, therapists model healthy conversation, emotional expression, and limit setting. This can be particularly important for people with BPD who have limited experience with good interactions.

Support and Encouragement: DBT coaches offer constant support and encouragement throughout your treatment process. They praise your successes and help you handle setbacks, creating a sense of hope and strength.

DBT goes beyond simply giving skills. It offers a thorough and open method specially developed to meet the difficulties of BPD. Through the mix of core principles, a complex treatment framework, and a focus on building a strong therapy relationship, DBT enables you to control your feelings effectively, foster healthy relationships, and build a more satisfying life. If you're dealing with BPD, DBT can be a useful tool on your path to mental well-being.

While Dialectical Behavior Therapy (DBT) gives you strong skills to control feelings and navigate relationships, another effective method for handling BPD is Cognitive Behavioral Therapy (CBT). This next part goes into the world of CBT, studying how to spot negative thought patterns that lead to emotional pain and learning useful tools for cognitive reform. By knowing how your thoughts impact your feelings, you can develop better-coping strategies and build strength in the face of difficulties.

CHAPTER 5

Cognitive Behavioral Therapy (CBT): Reshaping Thoughts and Behaviors

Our minds have great power. They have the power to affect our emotions and behaviors. We looked at dialectical behavior therapy (DBT) in the last chapter; it's a really useful toolkit for BPD patients to manage their relationships and emotions. This chapter explores Cognitive Behavioral Therapy (CBT), which is an additional useful strategy.

Here, we'll discover how, in certain cases, thoughts related to BPD might result in psychological distress. Fortunately, CBT provides useful methods and strategies to assist us in "rethinking" these unfavorable thought patterns. By comprehending the functioning of our minds, we can cultivate more constructive methods of managing obstacles and strengthen our emotional fortitude. Now let's explore CBT and discover the effectiveness of positive thinking!

Knowing the Influence of Thoughts

Our minds are very powerful. They serve as a kind of filter that shapes our perception of reality. They have an impact on our self-perception, our interpretation of the world, and ultimately, our emotions and actions. Negative thinking patterns can become engrained in BPD sufferers, resulting in emotional suffering and destructive behaviors.

Consider the following situation: When a close friend texts you briefly, you (having BPD) assume that they are upset with you right away. Anxiety, insecurity, and maybe even rage are some of the feelings that might be triggered by this unpleasant idea. This emotional high might drive you to behave rashly, like sending out a ton of texts demanding an explanation. This situation demonstrates the strong correlation that exists between ideas, feelings, and actions.

CBT is a potent management strategy for BPD. You will acquire important abilities to comprehend the relationship between your ideas and emotions via CBT. You can now confront your negative thought patterns and create more constructive coping strategies thanks to your increased awareness. You will thus be more capable of overcoming the difficulties caused by BPD.

Recognizing Adverse Thought Patterns

Recognizing these habitual negative beliefs is the first step. These warped mind patterns can occur so fast and subconsciously that they seem more like permanent realities than transient impressions. You can learn how these erroneous thought patterns start and how they exacerbate emotional suffering with the use of cognitive behavioral therapy (CBT). These negative thinking spirals and recurrent themes can be tracked using methods like journaling and mindfulness. You can confront these false ideas and open the door to a more powerful and balanced approach to managing BPD by realizing how these false beliefs contribute to emotional suffering.

The following techniques can be used to identify negative thinking patterns:

Be mindful of your feelings: When strong emotions, such as anger or worry, suddenly come to the surface, stop and consider the thoughts that led up to that feeling. Before you felt this way, what were you thinking?

How to recognize Negative thoughts and pay attention to emotions in an efficient manner

1. Acknowledge the Emotional Upswing:

Being aware of your emotional state throughout the day is the first step. Observe any abrupt changes in your mood, such as a pit in your stomach or a beating heart. These bodily experiences often indicate the onset of a strong emotion.

Example: Your supervisor abruptly summons you into their office while you're at work. Your hands begin to perspire, and you have a constriction in your chest.

2. Take a Moment to Think:

Pause and inhale for a second before responding hastily. You can become more conscious of your emotional condition during this little break so that you don't get sucked into it.

Example: Inhale deeply and permit yourself to go to the toilet for a little while.

3. Determine the Cause:

"What just happened before I felt this way?" ask yourself. Think back to any recent interactions, circumstances, or even inner thoughts that can have brought on the emotional change.

Example: Consider the unexpected call you received from your employer while using the toilet. Were you concerned about a recent project deadline?

4. Identify the Thought That Came Before:

Proceed further now. What was going through your head before the emotional outburst? You want to be able to recognize these habitual negative ideas.

For instance, you could have felt, "Oh no, what went wrong? I'm going to lose my job!" This kind of thinking can be traumatic.

It takes practice to use this procedure. It is easier to recognize the negative thinking patterns that fuel emotional pain the more you practice pausing to think.

• *Keep a mental journal:* Think of your ideas as ephemeral clouds that move across your consciousness. Many of these ideas, particularly the negative ones, might appear to come and go so fast that you hardly notice them. This is when journaling in CBT turns into your hidden weapon. This is how it operates:

• *Capture the Fleeting:* During the day, anytime you feel a wave of emotion coming on—such as grief, anger, or anxiety—take a minute to stop and pick up your diary. By pausing, you can catch those transitory unpleasant ideas that could otherwise pass by without your awareness.

• *Put it in writing:* Perfect wording and grammar are not important. Just write down the first thing that entered your head before the emotional outburst. Getting it "on paper" (or digitally) is essential for future analysis.

• *Context is Crucial:* Not only did the negative thinking surface, but also briefly describes the circumstances surrounding its emergence. Did that happen during a discussion? at the office? This background might provide important hints on possible causes.

• *Monitor Your Feelings:* After putting the idea on paper, make a note of the particular feeling you had (such as anger, anxiety, or sadness). It can be really enlightening to see the relationship between the idea and the feeling when it's written down.

• *Find Trends:* Go over your diary notes regularly. Do the negative ideas seem to have any recurrent themes? For instance, you may constantly experience feelings of abandonment or guilt. To challenge these habits in treatment, it is essential to recognize them.

You can learn a lot about your cognitive processes by regularly recording your feelings and ideas in a notebook. With improved emotional regulation and a more satisfying existence with BPD, you can work with your therapist in cognitive behavioral therapy (CBT) to establish more helpful and balanced thought patterns. This is made possible by your increased self-awareness.

5. Challenge the Evidence: When you recognize a negative idea, pose the following question to yourself: "Is this notion true? Exists proof to back that up?" These pessimistic ideas are often warped and unfounded in reality.

Let's say you sent an email with a typo by accident or made a little error at work. Suddenly, you're overcome with worry. You can be thinking something unpleasant, such as "I'm such a failure." I must be seen as inept by everybody." Remain still! CBT trains you to question the veracity of this thinking before allowing it to spiral. How to do it is as follows:

• *Examine the Correctness:* "Is this thought entirely accurate?" ask yourself. Is it really the case in this instance that one error makes everyone believe you are incompetent? Probably not.

• *Look for Proof:* Seek proof to confirm or disprove the unfavorable opinion. Is there a former situation when you received praise for your efforts from colleagues? Did the misspelling appear to especially annoy your boss?

Here are some more examples of combating pessimistic thoughts:

Scenario: Your buddy abruptly cancels the scheduled event.

Negative Idea: "It seems like they don't genuinely care about me." I'm alone myself."

Challenge: "Have they ever canceled plans for justifiable causes? Perhaps they're simply under stress. If they would want to reschedule, I can get in touch with them."

Situation: There's a party to which you are not invited.

Negative Idea: "I'm not liked by anybody. I'm uninteresting and lovable."

"Did everyone get an invitation? It could have been a little party. This weekend, I can arrange arrangements with other pals."

You might begin to recognize your negative ideas for what they often are—distorted perceptions driven by emotional distress—by questioning the facts that support them. This gives you the ability to create more realistic and balanced thought patterns, which in turn helps you feel less upset.

Common Negative Thought Patterns in BPD

The following are a few instances of typical negative thinking patterns that CBT might assist you with:

All-or-nothing perspective: exaggerated perceptions, such as "If I'm not perfect, I'm a complete failure." This can result in a severe dread of failing and trouble accepting errors.

Mind reading: This is the assumption that you are aware of the thoughts of others, often unfavorably. ("They must be thinking I'm boring.") This can exacerbate anxious and paranoid thoughts.

Catastrophizing: Blowing situations out of proportion and assuming the worst outcome. ("This text means they hate me and our friendship is over!") This can lead to anxiety and impulsive behaviors.

Emotional Reasoning: Believing your thoughts are facts. ("I feel worthless, therefore I must be worthless.") This can lead to negative self-esteem and self-deprecating behavior.

Personalization: Accepting responsibility for circumstances beyond your control. ("They're upset, it must be my fault.") Shame and guilt can increase as a result of this.

Cognitive Restructuring

Once you've discovered negative thought patterns, CBT provides you with real tools for "rethinking" them. This process, called cognitive retraining, includes questioning the truth of these negative thoughts and replacing them with more balanced and realistic ones.

Here's how brain restructuring works:

1. Identify The falsification:

The first step is noticing the specific type of negative thinking pattern hiding beneath your negative ideas. Here are some common misconceptions in BPD:

All-or-nothing thinking: Seeing things in extremes, with no room for fuzzy places. Example: You make a mistake at work by accidentally sending an email with a typo. A common all-or-nothing thought process in BPD might make you jump to this conclusion: "I'm a total failure. I'll never get anything right." (This ignores past wins and the chance of learning from the mistake.) This thought can feel true at the moment, but it's a skewed view driven by strong feelings.

Why is All-or-Nothing Thinking Problematic?

• *It Ignores Nuance:* This type of thinking sees things in extremes, leaving no room for the middle ground. A single mistake doesn't describe your entire worth or skill.

• *It Breeds Discouragement:* Believing you'll "never get anything right" stops you from trying again or learning from the experience.

• *It Fuels Emotional Distress:* These negative thoughts can cause extreme anxiety, shame, or anger, making it difficult to handle the situation effectively.

How to Challenge All-or-Nothing Thinking

• *Focus on proof:* Instead of dwelling on the negative thought, gather proof to the opposite. Have you gotten good comments on your work in the past? Can you learn from this mistake and improve next time?

• *Consider the range:* Instead of "failure" or "success," picture a range of performance. Everyone makes mistakes, and there's room for learning and growth.

• ***Develop a More Balanced Thought:*** Replace the all-or-nothing thought with a more realistic one. For example, "Everyone makes mistakes. This doesn't define me. I'll learn from it and do better next time."

Challenging negative thought patterns takes work. The more you question all-or-nothing thinking, the more you'll create a growth attitude and a better emotional reaction to losses.

Mind Reading: Assuming you know what others are thinking, often negatively. Example: Imagine you're having lunch with a friend, and they seem strangely quiet. Suddenly, a thought pops into your head: "They must be mad at me. I must have said something wrong." (This misses other reasons like your friend simply having a bad day.) This is a standard case of mind reading, a skewed thinking habit common in BPD. While it sounds true at the moment, it can lead to unnecessary worry and strain on relationships.

Why is Mind Reading Problematic?

• ***It Creates Insecurity:*** Constantly assuming you know what others are thinking (and that it's bad) can breed insecurity and make you question your interactions.

• ***It Fuels Emotional Distress:*** Believing someone is mad at you can cause worry, anger, or sadness, making it difficult to enjoy the moment.

• ***It Hinders Communication:*** Jumping to conclusions stops you from freely speaking with your friend to understand their true feelings.

How to Challenge Mind Reading

• ***Consider Alternative Explanations:*** Instead of thinking the worst, consider other options. Maybe your friend is having a bad day at work, or they're simply tired.

• ***Focus on Facts, Not Assumptions:*** Stick to what you can notice – your friend's quietness. Don't add your opinions without proof.

• ***Open Communication:*** The best way to know how someone feels is to ask them straight. Communicate freely and voice your concern: "Hey, you seem a little quiet today. Is everything alright?"

You don't have a mind-reading ability! Most people don't constantly overanalyze every encounter. By testing mind reading, you can develop better conversation skills and build stronger, more trusted partnerships.

Catastrophizing: Blowing events out of proportion and assuming the worst possible result. Example: Imagine you're expecting your partner home for dinner, but they run a few minutes late. A catastrophizing thought pattern, common in BPD, might make you jump to this conclusion: "They're probably in an accident. I'm all alone now." (This misses the chance of a simple traffic jam or a forgotten phone call.) This feels terrifying at the moment, but it's a skewed view driven by worry.

Why is Catastrophizing Problematic?

• *It Creates Unnecessary Distress:* Focusing on the worst-case scenario, however rare, leads to extreme worry, fear, and sadness.

• *It Impairs Rational Thinking:* When caught up in catastrophizing, it becomes difficult to think clearly and consider more practical options.

• *It Leads to Impulsive Actions:* Believing your partner is in danger might lead you to call them constantly or make foolish choices.

Challenging Catastrophizing

• *Examine the Probability:* Ask yourself, "How likely is this worst-case scenario to happen?" Car crashes are extremely rare, and your partner is likely just delayed.

• *Consider Alternative Explanations:* Instead of thinking the worst, brainstorm more likely reasons for their lateness. Traffic jam? Forgotten a phone call?

• *Develop Coping Mechanisms:* Develop good ways to handle worry while you wait. Try deep breathing routines, and awareness methods, or busy yourself with a calming task.

• *Speak effectively:* Once your partner comes, speak freely. Express your worry but avoid accusing words.

Most events have more possible answers than the worst-case scenario you dream up. By questioning these thoughts, you can develop a more balanced viewpoint, handle worry more effectively, and build better, more trusted relationships.

2. Challenge the Validity:

Once you've found the error, challenge the facts backing the negative thought. Ask yourself:

- Is this thought fully accurate?
- What proof supports this thought? What proof contradicts it?
- Are there different theories for the situation?

Here's how this works with the earlier examples:

All-or-Nothing Thinking:

Challenge: "Everyone makes mistakes. This doesn't define me. I can learn from it and do better next time."

Mind Reading:

Challenge: "I don't know for sure what they're feeling. Maybe they're just tired. I can always ask them straight if something's wrong."

Catastrophizing:

Challenge: "There are many reasons they could be late. I can try calling them to see if they're okay."

3. Develop a More Balanced Thought:

Finally, change the negative thought with a more fair and realistic one. This new thought should be:

• Exact: Focuses on the exact issue rather than assumptions.

• Evidence-Based: Supported by facts and evidence, not opinions.

• Helpful: Promotes a calmer mental state and more effective actions.

Here are some examples of more fair thoughts:

"I made a mistake, but I'm capable of learning and improving."

"I can't control other people's thoughts or feelings, but I can control my communication."

"There are many reasons why someone might be late. I'll wait a bit and then reach out if I haven't heard from them."

By constantly practicing cognitive restructuring, you gradually train your brain to think more healthily and helpfully. This enables you to control your feelings more effectively and face the challenges of BPD with greater confidence.

Learning Practical CBT Techniques

CBT offers a toolbox of useful tools to help you fight bad ideas and create healthy thinking patterns:

The ABC Model: This model helps you recognize the link between Activating Events (A), your Beliefs (B) about those events, and the resulting Consequences (C) (your feelings and actions). By reviewing your ideas, you can question their truth and build more flexible reactions.

• Activating Events (A): Situations or events that spark a response.

• Beliefs (B): Your ideas and opinions about those events.

• Consequences (C): The resulting feelings and actions you experience.

Scenario: You're at a social event and a group of people are laughing together. You feel a pang of sadness.

• A - Activating Event: Being at a social meeting while laughing.

• B - Belief: "Nobody here wants to talk to me. They must think I'm boring." (This is an example of mind reading and poor self-evaluation.)

• C - Consequences: Feeling sad and excluded. Maybe you remove yourself from the talk or avoid eye contact.

Writing and Analysis: By writing about these parts (A, B, C) and studying them, you can gain useful insights. Here's what writing might look like:

• Activating Event: Social meeting, people laughing in a group.

• Belief: I felt like nobody wanted to talk to me, that they think I'm boring.

• Consequences: I felt sad and withdrawn. I didn't join the chat.

Challenging the Belief:

The next step is to challenge the bad thoughts using CBT techniques:

• Is there evidence for my belief? Just because people were laughing doesn't mean they were excluding you. Maybe they were sharing an inside joke.

• Are there different explanations? Perhaps they're open to new discussions. Maybe you could approach them and introduce yourself.

• What is a more fair thought? "Not everyone will click with me at every event, but there are probably people here I could connect with."

Developing a More Helpful Response:

Instead of shrinking, you could try a more productive action based on reasonable thought:

• Approach a smaller group and introduce yourself.

• Find someone who seems friendly and ask a question about the event.

Carl's Example at Work:

Carl, a talented graphic artist, often experiences strong feelings at work. Recently, he got minimal comments on a project he poured his heart into. Let's see how the ABC Model can help him understand his emotional response:

• A - Activating Event: Carl gets his finished project back from his boss with minor input.

• B - Belief: "My work must not be good enough. I'm a bad planner, and everyone will think so now." (This is a mix of catastrophizing and poor self-evaluation.)

• C - Consequences: Carl feels a surge of worry and failure. He starts avoiding eye contact with peers and feels discouraged about starting his next job.

Journaling and Analysis: Carl chooses to use his CBT skills and writes about the situation:

• Activating Event: Received project back with minimal comments from the boss.

• Belief: My work must be bad. I'm a bad artist.

• Consequences: Feeling nervous and weak. Avoiding coworkers and feeling discouraged. Challenging the Belief: Now, Carl questions his negative belief using the methods learned in CBT:

• Is there evidence for my belief? Just because there weren't a lot of comments doesn't necessarily mean his work is bad. Maybe his boss is just busy.

• Are there different explanations? Perhaps his boss expects high quality from him and thinks he doesn't need specific comments this time.

• What is a more fair thought? "The lack of comments doesn't show my general skills. I can always explain standards or ask for more specific comments next time."

Developing a More Helpful Response: Instead of avoiding his boss, Carl decides on a more aggressive approach based on his balanced thoughts:

• Schedule a short meeting with his boss to discuss the project and get an explanation of the feedback.

• Ask if there are any specific areas he can improve on for future projects.

By using the ABC Model and questioning his bad views, Carl can build a more positive reaction to the situation. This allows him to control his nervousness, have a positive talk with his boss, and eventually improve his work. With the ABC Model and challenging bad ideas, you can also create more healthy thinking and helpful coping strategies. This enables you to handle social settings with greater confidence and control your feelings successfully. The ABC Model is a useful tool for self-awareness. The more you practice using it, the easier it will become to spot bad thought habits and create better ways of reacting to situations.

Journaling: Journaling is a cornerstone of CBT for BPD. It enables you to become a detective of your mind, discovering the secret patterns behind your emotional reactions. Our thoughts are often brief, moving through our minds like butterflies. Journaling helps you to record these thoughts before they disappear. Writing them down, even if it's messy or jumbled, helps you to see them for what they are: just thoughts, not necessarily facts. By regularly writing your ideas and feelings, you'll start to see repeating themes. For example, maybe you notice a pattern of negative self-criticism whenever you receive feedback, or perhaps you frequently have thoughts of leaving before social contact. Identifying these habits is important for addressing them in treatment.

The ABC Model and Journaling

The ABC Model (Activating Event, Belief, Consequence) is a useful tool in CBT. Journaling nicely supports the ABC Model by allowing you to track each element:

• Activating Event: Journal what happened that caused an emotional reaction. Be detailed about the event, the people involved, and any information you remember.

• Belief: Write down the thoughts that ran through your mind directly after the event. These are the unquestioned thoughts you want to examine.

• Consequence: Note the feelings you felt (anger, sadness, worry) and how you acted in response (withdrew, lashed out, etc.).

Here's an example of how writing might look with the ABC Model:

• Activating Event: My friend changed plans at the last minute.

• Belief: "They must not care about me. I guess I'm not important." (Mind reading and poor self-evaluation)

• Consequence: Feeling sad and ignored. Withdrew from social media and avoided reaching out to other friends.

Here are some writing questions specifically meant to help you spot bad thought patterns:

• What situations usually cause strong feelings for me? (e.g., criticism, rejection, feeling left out)

• What thoughts usually come to mind before I feel this way? (e.g., "I'm worthless," "Everyone hates me")

• Are these thoughts helpful or unhelpful? Why or why not? (Challenge the negative and create more healthy thinking)

As you regularly use writing in combination with CBT, you'll gain valuable self-awareness and create better thinking habits, eventually leading to a more satisfying life with BPD.

Behavioral Experiments: CBT advocates trying the truth of your bad thoughts. This can be a particularly strong tool for those with BPD who battle with catastrophizing or mind reading. For example, if you fear your friend is mad, you could reach out quietly and see how they react, rather than going to conclusions. By performing these tests, you can gather proof that challenges your negative views and build a sense of trust in your ability to handle relationships effectively.

Benefits of CBT for BPD

With CBT, you can learn to recognize and confront negative thinking patterns, which has several advantages:

1. Lessened Emotional Distress: Picture yourself being overcome by despair, rage, or worry as a result of erroneous reasoning. You can recognize these unfavorable ideas and refute them with the aid of CBT. You notice a marked reduction in the strength and occurrence of these debilitating feelings as you cultivate a more equilibrium viewpoint. More emotional stability and general well-being result from this.

2. Better Emotional Regulation: CBT gives you useful techniques to help you better regulate your emotions in addition to understanding them. You acquire good coping skills to comfort oneself in trying times. With the use of these abilities, you can control your emotions before they go out of control and cause impulsive acts or self-harm.

3. Enhanced Self-Esteem: BPD often results in a critical inner critic who feeds into unfavorable self-perceptions. You can learn to question these false beliefs about yourself using CBT. Your self-image becomes better when you recognize these false ideas and swap them out for more realistic, balanced ones. This cultivates an inner voice that is more welcoming and empathetic, which significantly raises your sense of confidence and self-worth.

4. Stronger Relationships: Picture having healthier, deeper connections with your loved ones. CBT gives you the tools you need to resolve conflicts amicably and effectively express your requirements. You acquire the skill of properly expressing your feelings while taking other people's viewpoints into account. Better communication builds understanding and trust, which strengthens and stabilizes relationships.

5. Greater Sense of Control: The sense of control that CBT provides is one of its most powerful features. You discover that your emotions and unfavorable ideas are not in control of you. With the help of CBT, you can learn to recognize these patterns and question them to replace them with more balanced ones. With this increased control, you can successfully manage your BPD symptoms and create a life that is meaningful and fulfilling.

You and your therapist can work together to implement CBT. Self-compassion and regular practice are necessary. There will be obstacles on your path, but if you work hard, you can learn to recognize and confront negative thinking patterns. In the end, CBT gives you the tools you need to control your BPD symptoms and create a life that is more emotionally stable, full of wholesome connections, and more cohesive with your identity.

Extra Advice for Using CBT Successfully

• *Find a Professional Therapist:* A licensed therapist can help you create coping methods that are customized to your requirements, provide individualized support, and mentor you through the CBT process.

• *Practice Makes Progress:* Consistent effort is necessary for CBT. It is easier to recognize and confront unpleasant ideas the more you practice doing so.

• *Have patience:* It takes time to break old mental habits. No matter how little your accomplishments can seem, acknowledge them and treat yourself with kindness as you go.

• *Focus on Progress Rather than Perfection:* Cognitive Behavioral Therapy (CBT) aims to foster better thought patterns rather than perfection. There will be moments when bad ideas attack. The secret is to recognize them and deal with them head-on.

Your BPD treatment plan can help you take charge of your ideas, learn to regulate your emotions, and create a more satisfying life by including cognitive behavioral therapy (CBT).

Now that you have the means to confront unhelpful thinking patterns, Chapter 6 shows you how to use these abilities in a therapeutic situation, such as psychotherapy. We'll look at several methods of treating BPD with psychotherapy, emphasizing the unique benefits of both individual and group treatment. You'll discover how a solid therapeutic alliance might enable you to address the underlying emotional needs influenced by your early life experiences, which are the source of your negative thought patterns. We'll also talk about Schema Therapy, a particular method that clarifies these events and any problematic coping strategies that can have grown out of them. By incorporating these realizations, you'll be even more prepared to create a life that is both balanced and rewarding.

CHAPTER 6

The Power of Psychotherapy: Building a Supportive Therapeutic Relationship

You now have strong skills for cognitive restructuring from Chapter 5, enabling you to recognize and question harmful thinking patterns. Although these abilities are essential for BPD management, implementing them in a way that lasts often necessitates a supportive setting. Now let's talk about psychotherapy.

The effectiveness of psychotherapy for BPD is examined in this chapter. We'll explore a range of therapeutic philosophies, each with its special insights and methods. However, a crucial component that unites all strategies is the therapeutic relationship, which offers support. The basis for an effective course of therapy is the trustworthy relationship that you have with your therapist. We'll talk about how this connection gives you the ability to confront your beliefs and take care of the underlying emotional needs that fuel your BPD symptoms. You will have a better knowledge of how psychotherapy can help you on your path to a more contented and balanced life by the conclusion of this chapter.

The Power of the Therapeutic Bond

Talk therapy, sometimes referred to as psychotherapy, provides a secure and private setting in which you can discuss your ideas, emotions, and experiences with a qualified mental health specialist. Although there are many different therapeutic philosophies, all of them are based on one essential component: a helpful therapeutic relationship. The foundation of an effective treatment plan is the trusting relationship that you have with your therapist.

Envision a lighthouse directing a vessel during a tempest. The therapist serves as a lighthouse for you, offering direction, encouragement, and a haven while navigating rough emotional waters. You will feel understood, acknowledged, and equipped to handle the challenges of borderline personality disorder via this partnership.

Although there are many different therapy modalities for BPD, one essential component unites them all: the supportive therapeutic alliance. The basis for a successful course of therapy is this connection. It's a relationship built on mutual respect, empathy, and a sincere desire to support you as you work through the challenges presented by BPD. In contrast to many relationships in your life, therapy provides a judgment-free environment. Your therapist's job is to understand your experiences and the underlying issues that underlie your BPD symptoms, not to judge or place blame on you. It can be quite therapeutic to be understood and appreciated. It offers a safe environment for you to examine your vulnerabilities by enabling you to let go of the weight of guilt and self-criticism.

Your therapist acts as a solid support while emotions are running high. They provide constant encouragement and support for the duration of your adventure. Honoring your accomplishments, no matter how minor keeps you motivated and bolsters your confidence in your capacity to recover. When you fall, they'll be there to catch you and give you a solid hand to get back up. The therapeutic alliance offers a secure haven where you can investigate your innermost emotions, ideas, and prior experiences. Your therapist provides a safe space for you to open up without worrying about being judged or ridiculed, whether you're talking about tough memories or facing tough feelings. You can learn more about the underlying reasons for your BPD symptoms as well as more about yourself via this investigation. BPD has the power to warp reality, leaving you feeling disoriented and perplexed. Your therapist helps you through the mist of skewed thinking by acting as a guide. They provide alternative viewpoints, dispel unfavorable ideas, and provide you with the tools you need to create a more accurate and balanced vision of the world and yourself.

You get an inner compass via the therapy interaction in addition to coping mechanisms. Your therapist gives you the skills and techniques you need to deal with obstacles on your own in the future. You can develop and gain control over your mental health with this increased feeling of strength and self-reliance. The therapeutic alliance has a beneficial effect that goes much beyond the treatment setting. Your life can change in unexpected ways when you enter treatment and feel empowered, understood, and supported. You can discover that you have better interpersonal connections, speak more clearly, and establish boundaries with more confidence. Therapy can equip you with the knowledge and abilities to face life's obstacles with more emotional maturity and resilience.

Exploring Different Paths: Therapeutic Approaches for BPD

Schema Therapy

Experiencing Borderline Personality Disorder (BPD) might be confusing. Feeling lost in a chaotic storm can be caused by intense emotions, rash decisions, and erroneous thought processes. Dr. Jeffrey Young's Schema Therapy (SFT) provides a strong compass to help you navigate these choppy seas.

SFT incorporates aspects of Gestalt therapy, psychodynamic theory, and cognitive-behavioral therapy (CBT) as well as other therapeutic philosophies. Schemas are a fundamental notion in SFT. See them as deeply rooted emotional and mental habits that developed throughout your early years, often as a result of unfulfilled desires or unhealthy family relationships. For instance, if you were abandoned often as a kid, you can grow up with an "Abandoned Child" schema, which can cause severe rejection anxiety and a strong need for intimacy.

These schemas influence your ideas, emotions, and actions subconsciously, much like subconscious blueprints. Even while they can have protected you as a kid, they can become maladaptive as adults, leading to serious problems and making it difficult for you to form wholesome connections.

The Five Schema Modes: Unmasking BPD's Complexity

SFT categorizes models into five main modes:

1. Abandoned and Abused Child: The Abandoned and Abused Child model in BPD can be a highly painful and widespread part of the illness. It's like having a hurt child living inside you, constantly seeking safety, love, and comfort. Here's a closer look at what this mode entails:

• ***Intense Fears of Abandonment:*** This is a core fear of the Abandoned and Abused Child. It might stem from real abandonment events in your childhood, such as a parent leaving the family, frequent mental abuse, or uneven parenting. You might become hypervigilant to signs of possible loss, misinterpreting neutral situations as rejection. This can lead to extreme worry, clinginess in relationships, or desperate attempts to hold onto people, even if it means sacrificing your own needs.

• *Feelings of Worthlessness:* The Abandoned and Abused Child often carries a deep sense of being unlovable and worthless. This might be a result of messages you got in your youth, such as criticism, neglect, or abuse. You might have a tough inner reviewer who constantly puts you down, leading to feelings of shame, low self-esteem, and trouble accepting praise or positive feedback.

• *Desperate Need for Love and Support:* This mode yearns for the love, safety, and care you could not have gotten as a kid. It can appear as a constant need for support, encouragement, and approval from others. You might favor others' needs over your own, afraid they will leave you if you share your wants. This can cause unhealthy dependence and trouble keeping healthy limits.

Impact on Your Life

The Abandoned and Abused Child model can greatly impact your life in different ways:

• *Relationships:* You might experience extreme jealousy, possessiveness, or clinginess in relationships due to the fear of loss. You might also fight with closeness due to the fear of being hurt again.

• *Emotions:* You might experience frequent anxiety, sadness, or emotional instability due to the fear of rejection and feelings of worthlessness.

• *Self-Esteem:* You might deal with low self-esteem and trouble making choices, constantly seeking outward support.

• *Self-Sabotaging Behaviors:* You might participate in self-sabotaging behaviors to push people away before they can leave you, fulfilling a self-fulfilling promise.

Healing the Abandoned and Abused Child

The good news is that the Abandoned and Abused Child model can be healed through therapy. Here are some strategies:

• *Cognitive Restructuring:* Learn to recognize and question negative thought processes about loss and self-worth.

• *Inner kid Work:* Connect with your inner kid and provide the love and support they never got.

• *Building Healthy connections:* Learn to build healthy, helpful connections with clear limits.

• *Developing Self-Compassion:* Cultivate self-compassion and learn to accept yourself with flaws.

Remember, the Abandoned and Abused Child is a part of you, but it doesn't define you. Through treatment and self-compassion, you can learn to soothe this sensitive part and create a better and more secure sense of self.

2. Angry Child: The Angry Child model in BPD is like having a part of you constantly stuck in a state of rage and frustration. It's a complicated mental state that can appear in different ways: The Angry Child is driven by a powerful mix of feelings like anger, hurt, rage, and unfairness. These feelings often stem from unmet wants and a sense of helplessness experienced in youth. You might have trouble sharing these feelings properly, leading to them building up and exploding in fits of rage or violence.

• *Impulsive Actions:* The Angry Child often acts abruptly, driven by strong feelings rather than reason. This can lead to saying or doing things you regret later, like making rash choices, self-harming, or participating in harmful behaviors.

• *Emotional Volatility:* Your feelings might feel like a wild ride with the Angry Child in control. You might experience fast mood swings, going from calm to angry in a matter of seconds, leaving yourself and those around you confused and disoriented.

• *Difficulty Managing Anger:* The Angry Child fights to control anger healthily. Traditional ways like bottling it up or acting out only make things worse. You might feel constantly on edge and easily triggered by imagined slights or insults.

Impact on Your Life

The Angry Child model can greatly impact your life in different ways:

• *Ties:* Your anger outbursts can hurt ties with friends, family, and love partners. People might feel like walking on eggshells around you, fearing your unstable anger.

• *Work and School:* Difficulties managing anger can harm your performance at work or school. Emotional outbursts or hasty decisions can risk your professional standing. •

Self-Esteem: Chronic anger can take a toll on your self-esteem. You might feel ashamed of your tantrums or rash actions, leading to a negative self-image.

• *Self-Harm:* In some cases, the Angry Child might turn to self-harm as a way to cope with overwhelming feelings.

Healing the Angry Child

The good news is that the Angry Child model can be controlled and soothed through treatment. Here are some strategies:

• *Identifying Triggers:* Learn to spot the events or people that cause your anger.

• *Healthy Expression of Anger:* Develop healthy ways to show your anger, such as aggressive conversation or physical exercise.

• *Emotional Regulation Skills:* Practice emotional regulation skills like awareness and relaxation methods to handle strong feelings before they increase.

• *Inner Child Work:* Connect with your inner Angry Child and understand the underlying hurt or frustration driving the anger.

Remember, the Angry Child is a part of you, but it doesn't control you. With treatment and self-awareness, you can learn to control your anger successfully and healthily share your feelings.

3. Punitive Parent: The Punitive Parent model in BPD is like having a persistent internal reviewer constantly judging and berating you. This harsh voice can be incredibly damaging to your self-esteem and general well-being. Here's a better look at this mode:

• *The Inner Critic Takes Center Stage:* The Punitive Parent acts as a dominating internal voice that constantly attacks your ideas, actions, and even your very being. This voice often echoes lessons you might have gotten from critical or harsh parents in your childhood. You might find yourself constantly second-guessing your choices, feeling like you're never good enough, and engaged in negative self-talk.

• *A Cycle of Self-Blame:* The Punitive Parent excels at blaming you for everything that goes wrong, even situations outside your control. This can lead to a persistent sense of guilt and shame, making it difficult to forgive yourself for mistakes. You might take criticism very personally; even small losses can start a flood of self-blame and negative self-evaluation.

• ***The Grip of Perfectionism:*** The Punitive Parent often sets overly high standards for yourself and others. This can appear as a dogged desire for greatness in everything you do. You might fight to accept your flaws, leading to anger, sadness, and self-punishment when you fall short of your own impossible standards.

• ***Self-Harmful Behaviors: In*** some cases, the excessive negativity of the Punitive Parent can lead to self-harm as a way to deal with the mental pain. This can be a dangerous way to handle tough feelings, and it's important to seek help if you find yourself turning to self-harm.

Impact on Your Life

The Punitive Parent model can greatly affect your life in different ways:

• ***Mental Health:*** The constant self-criticism and negativity can lead to worry, sadness, and low self-esteem.

• ***Relationships:*** You might fight to trust and accept love from others due to your poor self-image.

• ***Risk-Taking:*** The fear of failure taught by the Punitive Parent can lead to avoiding behaviors and trouble taking risks.

• ***Success:*** The chase of perfection can hinder your ability to enjoy the process of success and lead to a constant sense of inadequacy.

Healing the Punitive Parent

The good news is that the Punitive Parent model can be addressed and eased through therapy. Here are some strategies:

• ***Identifying the Critic:*** Learn to identify the voice of the Punitive Parent and separate it from your own good self-talk.

• ***Cognitive Restructuring:*** Challenge the negative and false beliefs pushed by the Punitive Parent with more balanced and caring self-talk.

• ***Setting practical Goals:*** Learn to set practical and doable goals for yourself, focused on growth rather than perfection.

- ***Developing Self-Compassion:*** Cultivate self-compassion and learn to accept yourself with all your flaws and faults.

- ***Inner Child Work:*** Connect with your inner child and understand the underlying emotional needs that might be driving the Punitive Parent's roughness.

Remember, the Punitive Parent may be part of you, but it doesn't have to rule you. With treatment and self-awareness, you can learn to stop the inner critic and create a more upbeat and helpful inner voice.

4. Detached Protector: The Detached Protector model in BPD is like having a built-in mental exit hatch. When faced with intense emotions, this mode kicks in, separating you from your feelings and experiences to numb the pain. While it might offer brief ease, it can have significant long-term effects. Here's a better look:

- ***Dissociation as a Coping strategy:*** The Detached Protector uses dissociation as its main protection strategy. Dissociation is a range of events where you separate from your ideas, feelings, memories, or sense of identity. You might experience daydreaming, feeling like a watcher in your own life, feeling mentally numb, or having gaps in your memory.

- ***A Shield Against Painful Emotions:*** The Detached Protector emerges when you view a situation as emotionally overwhelming. This could be caused by extreme joy, sadness, anger, or any strong feeling. By separating from your feelings, the Detached Protector protects you from emotional pain, but it also stops you from experiencing the full range of human emotions.

- ***Chronic Feelings of Emptiness:*** The constant emotional distance promoted by the Detached Protector can lead to a persistent sense of emptiness. This is because you're separated not only from bad feelings but also from good ones. You might feel a lack of drive, interest, or joy in life, feeling like you're going through the motions but not truly enjoying life.

Impact on Your Life

The Detached Protector model can greatly impact your life in different ways:

- ***Relationships:*** Your mental distance can make it difficult to connect with others on a deep level. People might view you as cold or uncaring.

• *Self-Esteem:* The constant nothingness and lack of emotional connection can lead to low self-esteem and a sense of isolation.

• *Daily Life:* Dissociation can affect your daily life, making it difficult to focus on chores or keep healthy habits.

• *Addiction:* In some cases, people with the Detached Protector model might turn to drugs or hobbies as a way to numb their feelings further.

Healing the Detached Protector

The good news is that the Detached Protector model can learn better coping strategies through treatment. Here are some strategies:

• *Grounding Techniques:* Learning grounding skills like mindfulness meditation or deep breathing exercises can help you reconnect with the present moment and handle overwhelming feelings.

• *Emotional Expression:* Developing skills for healthy emotional expression can help you process and release your feelings instead of putting them down.

• *Building Tolerance for Distress:* Learning to bear uncomfortable feelings without turning to withdrawal is key to emotional control.

• *Inner Child Work:* Connecting with your inner child and understanding the underlying fears or weaknesses that might be causing the Detached Protector.

5. Healthy Adult: In Schema Therapy (SFT), the Healthy Adult mode is the cornerstone of treatment. It reflects the part of you that aims for mental well-being, good relationships, and a satisfying life. Unlike the other schema modes, which are often reactive and led by past events, the Healthy Adult is an aware and aggressive force. Here's a deeper look at the traits of a strong Healthy Adult:

• *Emotional Regulation:* The Healthy Adult can spot and recognize your feelings without getting overpowered. It helps you control your emotional reactions and choose healthy ways to show or handle them. You can experience the full range of human emotions without feeling threatened or having to shut them down.

• *Healthy Coping Skills:* The Healthy Adult gives you with a toolbox of effective coping strategies to deal with stress, difficult situations, and strong feelings. This might include relaxing techniques, conversation skills, confidence, and problem-solving abilities. You can handle life's trials productively and happily.

• *Ability to Build Fulfilling Relationships:* The Healthy Adult fosters your ability to build and keep healthy relationships. It allows you to set limits, interact successfully, and engage in real emotional closeness with others. You can feel trust, respect, and equal support in your interactions.

• *Inner Defender and Wise Guide:* The Healthy Adult works as your inner defender, protecting you from manipulation and unhealthy interactions. It leads you toward making choices that are connected with your ideals and long-term well-being. You can approach life with a feeling of self-awareness, duty, and meaning.

Why is Strengthening the Healthy Adult Important?

SFT promotes developing the Healthy Adult mode because it enables you to take control of your life and handle your BPD symptoms. When the Healthy Adult is in charge, you can: • Challenge unhelpful schema beliefs: You can spot and challenge the skewed thinking patterns that add to your BPD symptoms.

• *Develop better relationships:* You can build and keep helpful relationships based on equal respect and trust.

• *Manage tough feelings:* You can learn to control your emotions properly without turning to rash behaviors.

• *Live a happy life:* You can follow your goals and dreams, having a greater sense of joy and happiness in life.

How to Strengthen the Healthy Adult

• *Therapy:* SFT therapists use different methods to help you improve your Healthy Adult mode. This might include role-playing healthy conversation skills, learning relaxation methods, and studying your core values.

• *Self-awareness:* Developing self-awareness is key. Notice when other schema modes are taking over and actively choose to trigger your Healthy Adult.

• *Self-Care:* Prioritizing self-care tasks like healthy eating, exercise, and getting enough sleep can greatly improve your mental well-being and strengthen your Healthy Adult.

The Healthy Adult is not an inborn trait, but rather a skill that can be grown with commitment and effort. By fostering your Healthy Adult, you can take care of your mental well-being and build a life filled with greater peace and meaning.

Re-parenting: Healing the Inner Child

One of the most unique aspects of SFT is the idea of re-parenting. This therapeutic process aims to meet the missing needs of your child's schemas through a caring and helpful therapy relationship. Imagine the therapist as a loving adult figure who provides the safety, support, and emotional connection you could have missed in your youth. By showing concern, giving encouragement, and setting healthy limits, the therapist helps you create a more positive mental picture of a helpful adult.

Beyond Re-parenting: A Multifaceted Approach

SFT uses a range of therapy methods to handle both the emotional and rational parts of BPD. Here are some key components:

Gestalt Techniques: Schema Therapy (SFT) uses Gestalt methods to bring your mental world to life. Imagine your mind as a stage where different parts of you, portrayed by the schema modes, play out their roles. Gestalt methods help you become the direction of this inner play, fostering a deeper understanding of how these modes combine and affect your behavior. Here's a closer look at how these methods are used in SFT:

• *Role-Playing:* Think of role-playing as a way to step into the shoes of different schema types. You might simulate a situation where, for example, the Abandoned Child feels ignored by a friend, and the Angry Child responds with anger. By actively playing these modes, you can gain a direct experience of their feelings, motives, and triggers. This helps you to watch how they connect and how they affect your general behavior.

• *Empty Chair Dialogues:* In this method, an empty chair represents a specific schema mode. You might sit facing the empty chair and participate in a chat, sharing your thoughts and feelings towards that mode, or vice versa. For instance, you might have a conversation with the Punitive Parent, questioning its sharp criticism and arguing for self-compassion. This allows you to face these mental opinions directly and begin to change their impact.

• *Visualization Exercises:* Visualization exercises tap into the power of your mind to explore schema modes and their effect. You might be led to imagine a safe place where you can communicate with different forms. For example, you might picture settling the

Angry Child with soothing images or giving comfort to the Abandoned Child. This allows you to practice better ways of connecting to these internal parts and create new coping strategies.

Benefits of Gestalt Techniques in SFT

• *Increased Self-Awareness:* By constantly interacting with your schema modes, you gain a better understanding of their causes, emotions, and motives. This self-awareness allows you to make conscious choices about how you respond to events.

• *Shifting Perspectives:* Gestalt methods allow you to see situations from the viewpoint of different schema modes. This promotes respect for yourself and helps you understand the root of your responses.

• *Developing Healthy Responses:* By practicing better relationships with your schema modes through role-playing and visualization, you can develop new coping strategies and emotional control skills.

• *Emotional Expression:* Gestalt methods can provide a safe space to address tough feelings connected with your schema modes, supporting emotional healing and release.

Overall, Gestalt methods in SFT are a powerful tool for bringing your inner world to light. By actively interacting with your schema modes, you can gain useful insights, question harmful habits, and eventually build a more integrated and durable sense of self.

Cognitive Restructuring: Schema Therapy (SFT) takes a useful tool from Cognitive Behavioral Therapy (CBT) called cognitive restructuring. This method focuses on finding and addressing the negative thought patterns that feed your mental discomfort and bad behaviors. Imagine these negative thoughts as skewed glasses through which you view the world. SFT helps you replace these lenses with a better viewpoint, promoting emotional control and a more cheerful attitude.

How Does Cognitive Restructuring Work in SFT?

• *Identifying Negative Thoughts:* The first step is to become aware of the negative natural thoughts that pop into your head in response to events or triggers. These ideas might be about yourself, others, or the world around you. For example, if the Abandoned Child mode is active, you might have the unconscious thought "Nobody cares about me" after a friend stops plans.

• *Evaluating the Evidence:* Once you've discovered a bad thought, SFT helps you analyze its truth. Is there real evidence to back this thought? Are there alternative, more fair reasons for the situation? In the above case, you might consider past instances where friends have shown they care, or admit that your friend might have a good reason for skipping.

• *Developing More Balanced Thoughts: The* next step is to question the negative idea and replace it with a more balanced and realistic one. This new thought should be based on facts and promote better emotional reactions. A more fair thought in the above situation could be "My friend must be busy, but they probably still care about me. I can try reaching out to change plans."

Benefits of Cognitive Restructuring in SFT

• *Reduced Emotional Distress:* By questioning negative thoughts, you can stop the loop of negative feelings they cause. This leads to a more upbeat mental state and better dealing with tough scenarios.

• *Improved Self-Esteem:* Challenging bad thoughts about yourself can improve your self-confidence and self-worth.

• *Enhanced Problem-Solving:* More balanced thought helps you to approach challenges and failures more effectively.

• *Reduced Risk-Taking Behaviors:* Challenging negative thoughts about loss or rejection can help you make better choices in relationships.

SFT therapists use different techniques to help you recognize and question bad thoughts. Some examples include:

• *Keeping a Thought Diary:* Tracking your bad thoughts and their effect on your feelings can show trends and help you spot cognitive distortions.

• *Socratic asking:* Therapists might ask questions to help you question the truth of your negative thoughts and explore alternative viewpoints.

• *Behavioral studies:* In some cases, therapists might urge you to perform studies to test the truth of your negative thoughts.

Cognitive retraining is an ongoing process. However, with constant effort and support from your therapist, you can learn to spot and question negative thought patterns, paving the way for a more balanced and mentally healthy life.

Assertiveness Training: BPD can often lead to problems in conversation. You might struggle to explain your wants clearly, leading to anger and hostility. Conversely, you might turn to violence or trickery to get your needs met. This is where confidence training in SFT comes in. It gives you the skills to handle conversation difficulties and build better relationships. Assertiveness training is a set of communication skills that help you share your ideas, feelings, and wants in a clear, honest, and polite way. It's about finding a balance between being quiet and active. Here are some key parts of confidence training in SFT:

• *Identifying Your Needs:* The first step is to become aware of your wants and goals in a given scenario. What do you want to achieve through communication?

• *Clear and Direct Communication:* Assertiveness training teaches you how to voice your wants clearly and directly, using "I" statements. For example, instead of saying "You never listen to me," you could say, "I feel ignored when you stop me. Could you please let me finish?"

• *Setting limits:* Healthy limits are important for protecting your well-being in partnerships. Assertiveness training helps you set limits and express them successfully. For example, you might learn to say no to ridiculous requests or politely excuse yourself from stressful situations.

• *Active Listening:* Assertiveness is a two-way street. SFT includes active listening skills to help you truly understand the other person's view while fighting for your own needs.

• *Nonverbal Communication:* Assertiveness goes beyond words. Maintaining eye contact, using a confident body position, and speaking with a clear, calm voice all add to successful communication.

Benefits of Assertiveness Training in SFT

• *Improved Communication:* By learning to explain yourself clearly and respectfully, you can build better, more enjoyable connections.

• *Reduced Conflict:* Assertiveness skills can help you manage differences and conflicts effectively, reducing drama and anger.

• ***Increased Self-Esteem:*** Learning to fight for yourself and having your needs met can greatly improve your self-confidence and sense of self-worth.

• ***Reduced Reliance on Schema Modes:*** When you have effective communication skills, you're less likely to turn to unhealthy coping strategies connected with your schema modes, like manipulation or violence.

Putting confidence into Practice: SFT therapists use different methods to help you build confidence skills. Here are a few examples:

• ***Role-Playing:*** Practicing bold conversation in imagined situations helps you to try and build confidence.

• ***Identifying Communication Styles:*** Learning to spot your communication style and those of others can help you tailor your approach for more effective interaction.

• ***Developing "I" Statements:*** Therapists can help you in creating clear and short "I" statements that describe your wants and feelings without blaming or judging the other person.

Assertiveness is a skill that takes time and practice to improve. However, with constant effort and the direction of your SFT therapist, you can learn to express your needs successfully and build better, more enjoyable partnerships.

The Importance of the Therapeutic Relationship and Boundaries

In SFT, the therapeutic relationship is central to the therapy process. By creating a secure and supportive atmosphere, the therapist encourages you to examine your weaknesses and try out better ways of being. SFT therapists can be more open than typical therapists, disclosing pertinent personal details in a controlled setting to demonstrate healthy vulnerability and emotional expression. However, keeping clear therapeutic boundaries is critical to avoid blurring the lines between therapist and friend/parent.

Considerations and Cautions

Even though SFT is a very effective method for treating BPD, there can be some difficulties. Re-parenting can be a very emotional process, and therapists need to be quite adept at handling transference and countertransference problems. It's critical to maintain a supportive and competent therapy connection while steering clear of situations that might cause you to experience trauma again.

Through the integration of ideas from other therapeutic philosophies, SFT provides a thorough method for treating BPD. You can start a transforming path towards emotional healing and more satisfying life by recognizing and confronting problematic schemas, re-parenting the wounded child inside, and learning new coping mechanisms. Recall that you are not defined by BPD. You can learn to control your symptoms and create a life that is more emotionally stable and peaceful with the correct resources and assistance.

Mentalization-Based Therapy (MBT)

Picture having the ability to see your thoughts and emotions from a distance, as if you were viewing a self-produced film. This is the fundamental idea behind the word "mentalization," which was coined by psychologist Peter Fonagy. Understanding how your mind works, how other people's minds function, and how these internal landscapes affect how you interact with the outside world is the essence of mentalization. Consider it as having an interpreter for human behavior built right in. You can comprehend why you and other people behave in certain ways if you have great mentalization abilities. This helps you become more self-aware while also enabling you to understand other people's motives and emotions.

Two more crucial abilities are strongly related to this idea:

• *Psychological Mindfulness:* This is the capacity to recognize the relationship between your feelings, ideas, and actions. It's about realizing how your inner world influences the things you do.

• *Mindfulness:* This means focusing on the here and now without passing judgment. It enables you to be aware of your emotions and ideas without allowing them to consume you.

According to Fonagy, early childhood disruptions to this normal mentalization process might have a role in the development of personality disorders, especially borderline personality disorder (BPD), later in life.

Here's how this interruption might occur: You can lack

Problems with Attachment: A stable and sound bond with a caregiver is essential for a child's emotional growth. Your capacity to comprehend and control your own emotions can be hampered if this relationship is broken by abuse, neglect, or even overbearing parenting. It's possible that you lack a sound foundation for understanding how you feel about yourself or how other people behave.

Object Coherence: This is the capacity to keep a mental picture of a person you care about even when they are not there in person. A person with BPD can have difficulties with object constancy when attachment is disturbed, clinging to connections out of fear of being abandoned, or, on the other hand, completely withdrawing emotionally from other people.

There are many possible reasons for these development disruptions:

Temperament: Some people can be biologically or genetically predisposed to struggle with mentalization.

Parenting Issues: A child's capacity to acquire sound mentalization techniques might be hampered by parental characteristics such as physical or emotional abuse, neglect, or even excessively controlling conduct.

How MBT Can Help

MBT works on the premise that to be as effective as possible in relationships, you must first be able to comprehend the beliefs, motives, feelings, wants, and reasoning of both yourself and other people. Although studies on MBT's efficacy are still being conducted, preliminary findings from Bateman and Fonagy's study have been encouraging. An example of a standard MBT program is as follows: You will typically participate in the program in a daily partial hospitalization environment, attending treatment most weekdays for a minimum of eighteen months.

Therapy Components: The program includes several components, including:

- ***Psychoanalytically Oriented Group Therapy:*** This kind of group therapy offers a secure atmosphere for practicing mentalization techniques and examining interpersonal dynamics.

- ***Individual Psychotherapy:*** With your therapist's help, you can explore your challenges in more detail and create coping strategies during individual sessions.

- ***Expressive Therapies:*** Psychodrama, music, and art can provide a variety of creative outlets for emotional experience inquiry and self-expression.

• *Medication:* When required, medication can be used to treat mental health disorders including sadness and anxiety that co-occur.

• *Collaboration among Staff:* Regular staff meetings guarantee treatment continuity and provide therapists with a safety net for challenging situations.

MBT-trained therapists use a manualized method that focuses on your present mental state. They support you in seeing the distortions in your views of other people and yourself and in working together to create new, more impartial viewpoints. While MBT has a stronger basis in psychodynamic theory, akin to Transference-Focused Psychotherapy (TFP), it also shares certain strategies with other treatments, such as Dialectical Behavior Therapy (DBT), in terms of developing behavioral skills.

Gaining mastery over mentalization techniques helps you understand yourself and others around you better. This gives you the ability to better manage the symptoms of BPD, mend your relationships, and navigate your emotions. Recall that MBT is a path of self-discovery. With commitment and your therapist's help, you can create a life that is more emotionally balanced and meaningful.

Interpersonal Therapy (IPT)

Unlike some treatments that dig deeper into your past, IPT focuses mainly on your present situation. It recognizes that past events can influence your present, but the major focus is on finding and solving the relationship problems that are currently causing you pain. IPT gives you a set of useful tools to manage the difficulties of relationships. Here are some key areas of focus:

• *Communication Skills:* Strong conversation is the basis of healthy interactions. IPT teaches you skills like active listening, voicing your wants assertively, and settling disagreements productively.

• *Conflict Resolution:* Disagreements are expected in any relationship. IPT gives you methods for handling problems quietly, expressing your perspective clearly, and finding solutions that work for everyone involved.

• *Building and Maintaining Relationships:* Whether it's friendships, love relationships, or family bonds, IPT guides how to build and support healthy ties. You'll learn how to set healthy limits, show love properly, and handle the complexities of social contact.

Addressing Current Life Stressors: Life can throw curveballs, and stressful events can worsen BPD symptoms. IPT sees this and helps you spot present stresses that might be adding to your mental discomfort. Here's how:

Identifying Stressors: The therapist works with you to find the specific stresses in your life, such as job challenges, relationship problems, or cash fears.

Developing Coping Methods: Once the stresses are discovered, IPT provides you with coping methods to handle them successfully. These might include stress management methods like relaxing routines, conversation skills to handle the cause of stress, or problem-solving strategies to face obstacles.

Benefits of IPT for BPD

By handling your current relationship problems and providing you with effective conversation and coping skills, IPT can lead to several positive outcomes:

• ***Reduced Emotional Distress:*** Improved conversation and relationship management can greatly reduce stress and emotional instability, leading to a greater sense of calm and well-being.

• ***Enhanced Self-Esteem:*** Building better relationships can boost your self-confidence and sense of worth.

• ***Stronger Support System:*** With better communication and conflict resolution skills, you can build stronger, more helpful relationships with loved ones.

• ***Reduced Reliance on Unhealthy Coping Mechanisms:*** IPT enables you to handle difficult feelings and face difficulties safely, reducing the need for unhealthy coping mechanisms that are often seen in BPD.

IPT utilizes a joint method where you and the therapist work together to discover your goals and create tactics for achieving them. Here are some examples of how therapy might unfold:

Identifying Interpersonal trends: The therapist might help you spot trends in your interactions, for example, how you speak with others or how you respond to disagreement.

Role-Playing: Practicing conversation skills and conflict resolution methods in a safe, controlled setting can build confidence and improve your ability to apply these skills in real-life scenarios.

Homework Assignments: The therapist might give homework tasks to encourage you to apply the skills learned in therapy to your daily exchanges.

Individual vs. Group Therapy: Tailoring Treatment to Your Needs

Psychotherapy can take place in a group or individual context. Both have distinct advantages:

- Individual therapy gives you and your therapist a quiet place to thoroughly discuss your emotions and views. Therapy can be customized to meet your unique requirements and objectives.
- Provides a feeling of connection and community via group therapy. In a secure and encouraging setting, you can confront harmful ideas, build coping methods with others who have BPD, and learn from and support one another.

Advantages of a Therapeutic Supportive Relationship

Numerous advantages of the therapeutic alliance might support you as you go toward healing:

Acceptance and Validation: Effective treatment starts with you feeling understood and accepted for who you are, without judgment. It can be very uplifting and comforting to get this confirmation.

Encouragement and Support: Your therapist will act as your rallying point, praising your accomplishments and offering assistance when things become tough. Maintaining your motivation and dedication to your treatment objectives can depend on this.

A Confidential and Safe Environment for Exploration: Therapy offers an environment where you can freely explore your ideas, emotions, and experiences without worrying about being judged. When processing challenging emotions and painful memories, can be really beneficial.

Advice and Insight: Your therapist will provide advice, insights, and many viewpoints to assist you get a better understanding of your BPD and yourself. With this newfound knowledge, you can effectively manage your symptoms.

Creating Healthy Coping Strategies: To manage emotional discomfort, enhance communication, and forge stronger bonds with others, your therapist will work with you to discover and create healthy coping strategies.

BPD often results from early life events that might have made you feel unwanted, insecure, or abandoned. These encounters have the power to mold your fundamental ideas about the world and about yourself, as well as to encourage the formation of undesirable coping strategies. You can examine these early events in a secure and encouraging setting via therapy. You can start to get beyond the past and create a more rewarding future by realizing your emotional needs and the causes of your unfavorable thinking patterns.

Understanding STEPPS: A Comprehensive Program for Borderline Personality Disorder

STEPPS is a group-based teaching program created by Nancee Blum, MSW, and is intended to be used in conjunction with individual treatment and medication for those with BPD. It's regarded as a "value-added" treatment since it complements existing therapy rather than completely replacing it. The three main objectives of the program are:

Psychoeducation: The goal of STEPPS is to teach BPD to patients and the people who support them, such as friends, family, and therapists. With this understanding, everyone concerned can better assist the patient's healing process and have a better understanding of the situation.

Skill Development: The goal of STEPPS is to provide patients with the tools they need to control their emotions and regulate their behavior. These abilities enable people with BPD to better control their emotions and react in healthy ways to difficult circumstances.

For BPD rehabilitation, the approach emphasizes the critical significance that a robust support network plays. STEPPS offers techniques and resources to improve interaction and cooperation between the patient and the people in their support system.

Evidence-Based efficacy: There is a growing amount of research that supports the efficacy of STPPS, giving it a solid scientific base. Research has shown that the program can significantly lessen symptoms of BPD;

This implies that STEPPS can lessen the strain on healthcare systems in addition to enhancing patients' mental health.

Although STEPPS was first created in the US, it has now spread to other nations, such as the Netherlands. This indicates that it can be used more broadly and adjusted to other cultures. BPD is seen by STEPPS as an emotional and behavioral regulation disorder. The program is designed to address these core symptoms and offer comprehensive support for emotional well-being. It acknowledges that individuals with BPD can have difficulties with:

• Managing intense emotions

• regulating their behavior

• Experiencing distorted perceptions and thought patterns (e.g., splitting, all-or-nothing thinking).

In contrast to Other Therapies:

The creators of STEPPS point out the benefits of their program over other well-liked BPD therapies, such as Mentalization-Based Therapy (MBT) and Dialectical Behavior Therapy (DBT). Below is a summary of the main ideas:

Time Commitment: DBT can take a lot of time since it calls for regular individual treatment sessions as well as skill development. STEPPS provides weekly group sessions at a more reasonable time commitment.

Therapist Qualifications: Individual therapy and skills training in DBT must be provided by therapists who have received specialized training in the technique. This might put patients in a position where they have to see a different therapist to obtain DBT, which could disrupt their established therapeutic alliance. The patient's current therapist's continuing individual treatment and STEPPS combine harmoniously.

Accessibility and Resources: Due to a shortage of licensed therapists in certain places, DBT and MBT can not be widely accessible. Furthermore, these treatments can be quite demanding on therapists, necessitating a large time and training commitment. STEPPS provides a more approachable choice for therapists and patients alike.

In summary, STEPS offers a useful therapeutic strategy for BPD. With an emphasis on skill building, psychoeducation, and bolstering support networks, it offers a thorough framework for addressing the fundamental issues associated with BPD. STEPPS has accessibility benefits and is evidence-based, making it a valuable tool for BPD sufferers and the networks that support them as they progress toward recovery.

Identifying Unhealthy Coping Mechanisms

Being self-aware is the first step in making a good change. Here's how to recognize harmful coping strategies in your life:

• ***Recognize Emotional Stressors:*** Keep an eye out for circumstances or feelings that usually set off your BPD symptoms. What experiences or emotions make you turn to harmful coping techniques?

• ***Monitor Your Actions:*** After you've identified your triggers, keep an eye on how you react to them. How do you handle the intense emotional state?

• ***Take Into Account the Long-Term Effects:*** Consider, "Does this coping mechanism truly help me in the long run, or does it create more problems?" For instance, abusing drugs or alcohol can provide a momentary reprieve from mental distress, but in the long run, it causes interpersonal difficulties and health issues.

The following are a few typical problematic coping techniques linked to BPD:

• ***Self-harm:*** intentionally causing oneself pain as a coping mechanism for intense feelings.

• ***Substance abuse:*** Abusing alcohol or drugs to cope with emotional distress or get out of sticky situations.

• ***Compulsive Behaviors:*** Taking action on the spur of the moment without thinking through the repercussions, including careless spending or unsafe sexual activity.

• ***Emotional Eating:*** When people use food as a coping mechanism for unpleasant feelings, they tend to consume unhealthy foods.

• ***Withdrawal or Isolation:*** Removing oneself from social interactions, family, and friends to protect one's emotions.

• ***Threatening self-harm or suicide:*** Making threats to control others or attract attention.

Creating Well-Being Adult Coping Strategies

The good news is that you can successfully control your BPD symptoms by learning and developing healthy coping methods. The Healthy Adult schema mode steps in at this point. According to The Power of the Healthy Adult, the Healthy Adult mode is the aspect of you that aspires to emotional stability, wholesome relationships, and sound decision-making. You can develop more constructive coping mechanisms for dealing with emotional difficulties by enhancing this mode.

Changing Bad Habits: After you've recognized your harmful coping strategies, you can swap them out for more beneficial ones. Although it will take some time and work, you can form new habits that support emotional control and well-being via regular practice.

The following are some instances of constructive coping strategies you might adopt:

• *Mindfulness and Relaxation Techniques:* You can control your emotional intensity and achieve a feeling of peace by engaging in mindfulness and relaxation techniques including progressive muscle relaxation, deep breathing exercises, and meditation.

• *Emotional Expression:* Talking to a therapist or trusted friend can help you express your feelings in a healthy manner, which is a valuable tool for managing emotional pain.

• *Distraction Techniques:* When feeling overwhelmed, partaking in enjoyable activities such as exercising, going on a nature walk, or listening to music can serve as a healthy diversion and lessen the severity of your emotions.

• *Creating Healthy Relationships:* A safe place to express yourself and get emotional support can be found in a network of friends, family, or a therapist.

• *Self-Care:* It's essential for general well-being to give top priority to things that feed your body, mind, and soul, such as eating a balanced diet, getting adequate sleep, and pursuing hobbies.

• *Dialectical Behavior Therapy:* (DBT) is a thorough skills training program that gives you the tools you need to effectively manage your emotions, tolerate discomfort, interact with others, and practice mindfulness.

While treatment is essential for controlling borderline personality disorder, a comprehensive strategy often produces the greatest outcomes. We will discuss how dietary support and pharmaceutical concerns might complement treatment to further empower you on your path to emotional well-being in the next chapter. In order to treat certain BPD symptoms, Chapter 7 explores the possible advantages of several drugs, such as mood stabilizers, antipsychotics, antidepressants, and anxiety reducers. We'll also discuss how nutrition and supplements might support neurotransmitter balance and perhaps help you feel more emotionally stable. You can develop a complete management strategy that promotes improved emotional control and general well-being by combining these various techniques.

CHAPTER 7

Beyond Therapy: Integrative Approaches for BPD Medications

Even while psychotherapy has long been a mainstay in discussions about managing Borderline Personality Disorder (BPD), it's crucial to understand that there are often several steps on the path to emotional well-being. This chapter examines a comprehensive strategy for managing BPD, going beyond the confines of treatment alone. We'll explore complementary techniques that can support treatment in a way that will enable you to move toward improved emotional stability and general well-being.

Here, we'll discuss the possible advantages of certain medications that can be used to treat particular BPD symptoms, such as mood stabilizers, antipsychotics, antidepressants, and medications for anxiety. We'll also discuss the intriguing relationship between diet and brain chemistry. We are going to examine how nutrition and supplements support neurotransmitter balance to learn how dietary decisions can be linked to emotional stability. This chapter gives you the information you need to think about a thorough management strategy that incorporates several different techniques. You can empower yourself to develop higher emotional control and create a more peaceful, balanced existence by combining these many tactics with treatment.

Even though therapy is the mainstay of treatment, taking medication can be a very useful ally on the path to emotional recovery. We'll look at two main justifications for drug usage in BPD therapy here.

Imagine attempting to construct a home on a sand foundation that is constantly changing. Building a strong, solid building is not easy. Similarly, emotional dysregulation might make it difficult for you to participate completely in treatment if you have BPD. Drugs can reduce the frequency and severity of mood swings, resulting in a more stable emotional state. This makes it easier for you to concentrate during treatment sessions and to take an active role in picking up new coping skills. Emotional upheaval can impair your judgment and make it hard to focus. Medications can help you concentrate, digest information more easily, and come to logical conclusions. This improved cognitive function enables you to comprehend and use the therapeutic methods more effectively. You can engage in more pleasant and productive interactions with others when your emotional state is more stable. This can reduce tension and provide a more encouraging atmosphere for you to forge greater bonds with your therapist and loved ones.

Taking Care of Co-Occurring Conditions

BPD and other mental health issues including anxiety, depression, or ADHD often co-occur. Drugs can more successfully address the distinct symptoms of various co-occurring disorders, allowing for a more all-encompassing approach to treating your mental health in general.

Because they are unable to manage their emotions, many people with BPD experience feelings of guilt and self-blame. They can think that their actions are a reflection of weakness or a personal flaw. Medication can help you see that your conduct is not a personal failing but rather the outcome of the underlying problem by reducing the severity of your symptoms. You can develop self-compassion and empathy for the difficulties you encounter with less emotional upheaval. This change in viewpoint might enable you to concentrate on development and healing. Medication makes it possible for you to engage fully in treatment and pick up useful coping skills. With your newly acquired emotional intelligence, you can end the vicious cycle of self-destructive behavior and create a more satisfying existence.

Exploring Treatment Options for Borderline Personality Disorder

Antipsychotics and Atypical Antipsychotics

A Historical Perspective: First-Generation Antipsychotics (FGAs)

The initial study of medicines for BPD started with a class known as neuroleptics, now referred to as first-generation antipsychotics (FGAs). These drugs, including chlorpromazine (Thorazine), trifluoperazine (Stelazine), and haloperidol (Haldol), were initially made for treating serious mental diseases like schizophrenia and bipolar disorder. Their success came from their ability to stop a specific brain receptor called the dopamine

D2 receptor. While this mechanism produced therapeutic effects, such as reducing hallucinations and delusions, it also, unfortunately, led to a range of side effects, most notably movement disorders like acute dyskinesias (involuntary muscle contractions) and tardive dyskinesia (involuntary repetitive movements that typically develop after long-term use). Seeking to solve the limits of FGAs, researchers created a new class of drugs called atypical antipsychotics (SGAs), also referred to as second-generation antipsychotics. This group, including clozapine (Clozaril), olanzapine (Zyprexa), risperidone (Risperdal), quetiapine (Seroquel), aripiprazole (Abilify), lurasidone (Latuda), brexpiprazole (Rexulti), and others, gave several benefits over FGAs.

Reduced Side Effects: Notably, SGAs looked to have a lower chance of causing movement problems compared to FGAs. This is because they often have a different mode of action, affecting not only the dopamine D2 receptor but also the serotonin 5HT2A receptor. This larger action might add to their efficiency and possibly lessen side effects.

Improved Symptom Targeting: While FGAs were mainly created for treating mental symptoms, SGAs might have a wider effect on some of the core symptoms of BPD, such as emotional instability and recklessness.

While studies on drugs for BPD are ongoing, a growing amount of data shows the possible benefits of SGAs in treating specific BPD symptoms. Here's a breakdown of some key findings:

Meta-analyses (studies that examine the results of multiple clinical trials) suggest that SGAs like aripiprazole (Abilify), haloperidol (Haldol), and olanzapine (Zyprexa) might help lower signs of emotional instability, hyperactivity, and cognitive problems. These studies show that SGAs can help people with BPD experience a more calm mental state, make more reasonable choices, and improve their ability to focus and process information.

Studies on Olanzapine (Zyprexa): This particular SGA has been widely studied in BPD treatment. While one big study met the standards for FDA approval for BPD, another fell short by a small margin. Despite this, olanzapine remains a widely used drug due to the strong data backing its effectiveness in lowering symptoms like anger, irritability, and emotional instability.

Quetiapine (Seroquel): A 2014 study by Dr. Donald Black shows that quetiapine, at specific doses (150mg and 300mg per day), might be better than a placebo in controlling

BPD symptoms. Interestingly, the study found a possibly bigger benefit at lower doses, showing that lower amounts might be just as useful with fewer side effects.

Lurasidone (Latuda): While the study on lurasidone especially for BPD is limited, some doctors describe hopeful results, particularly due to its good side-effect profile compared to other SGAs. However, more study is needed to determine its success in BPD treatment.

Important Considerations: Side Effects and Individualized Treatment

While SGAs give promise, it's important to be aware of possible side effects:

• ***Weight Gain:*** This is a frequent side effect linked with some SGAs, especially olanzapine (Zyprexa).

• ***Metabolic Changes:*** These drugs might raise blood cholesterol and prolactin levels, and possibly lower glucose tolerance, which can impact diabetes control. Regular tracking by your doctor is crucial to reduce these risks.

• ***Sedation:*** Some SGAs can cause sleep, which can be a problem for some people.

Individualized Treatment and Medication Selection

Finding the right medicine for BPD is a highly unique process. Here's what you can expect when working with your psychiatrist:

• Your doctor will perform a full exam to understand your unique symptoms, medical background, and any other drugs you might be taking.

• There's no "one size fits all" method to medicine for BPD. Your therapist will consider your unique wants and tastes when choosing a drug and amount.

• It might take some time to find the medicine that works best for you. Your doctor will likely suggest starting with a low amount and gradually increasing it as needed while watching for usefulness and side effects. Open communication throughout this process is important.

• BPD often co-occurs with other mental health problems like sadness, anxiety, or ADHD. Medications can be particularly helpful in treating these co-occurring conditions, leading to a more thorough approach to managing your general mental health.

While medicine can be a useful tool, it's important to remember it's just one piece of the picture in BPD care. Psychotherapy remains the cornerstone of treatment, as it gives you the skills to control your feelings, regulate behavior, and build healthy relationships. Additionally, lifestyle changes such as regular exercise, good sleep habits, and stress management methods can play a significant role in your general well-being.

Addressing Common Concerns: Tardive Dyskinesia (TD) and Off-Label Use

Tardive Dyskinesia (TD): Some people might be nervous about taking antipsychotics due to worries about tardive dyskinesia (TD). This is a movement disease that can emerge with long-term use of high-dose antipsychotics, especially FGAs. However, the study on SGAs used in BPD treatment is encouraging. The risk of TD looks to be greatly lower compared to FGAs, especially in smaller amounts. It's important to share any worries you might have with your therapist, and they will watch you for any possible signs of TD.

Off-Label Use: As stated earlier, olanzapine (Zyprexa) is not officially FDA-approved for BPD. However, doctors can recommend medicines for reasons other than their FDA-approved indications, which is referred to as "off-label use." This approach is common when there is strong evidence backing the success of a drug for a particular condition, even if it hasn't gotten official FDA approval for that specific use. Your doctor will share the risks and benefits of off-label use with you so you can make an informed choice.

Borderline Personality Disorder can be a difficult condition, but with the right treatment method, you can experience major growth and live a happy life. Medication, when used properly alongside treatment and healthy living choices, can be a powerful tool in your healing process. By working closely with your healthcare team, you can explore your treatment choices and create a personalized plan that allows you to control your symptoms and achieve mental well-being. Remember, healing is a process, and there will be ups and downs along the way. However, with commitment and help, you can build a better future.

Mood Stabilizers: Exploring Antiepileptic Options in Borderline Personality Disorder Treatment

The Link Between Epilepsy and BPD: Targeting a Shared Neural Region

The use of antiepileptic drugs in BPD treatment stems from an interesting link between the two illnesses. Research shows that many people with BPD display problems in the middle temporal parts of the brain. This area, which includes the amygdala and the anterior cingulate cortex, plays a key part in controlling feelings and behavior. Interestingly, this same brain area is also involved in complicated partial seizure disorders, a type of epilepsy.

The Amygdala: Research shows that the amygdala, responsible for handling feelings like fear and anger, might be elevated in people with BPD. This can lead to heightened emotional reactions and trouble managing feelings.

The Anterior Cingulate Cortex: On the other hand, the anterior cingulate cortex, which helps us control behavior and make choices, might be less involved in BPD. This can lead to recklessness and trouble with mental control.

Antiepileptic drugs, created to control seizure behavior, can also have a good effect on these brain areas in BPD. By possibly slowing down overactivity in the amygdala and improving the function of the anterior cingulate cortex, these drugs might contribute to better emotional control and decreased recklessness.

Neurotransmitter Imbalances and Potential Benefits

The success of antiepileptic drugs in BPD might also be explained by their effects on nerve systems.

Glutamate and GABA: These are the brain's major stimulating and inhibitory chemicals, respectively. Research shows that people with BPD might have abnormal amounts and activity of these chemicals. Antiepileptic drugs can work by changing the activity of these chemicals, possibly leading to a more normal brain chemistry and better emotional control.

Dopamine and Serotonin: While antipsychotics mainly target these chemicals, some antiepileptic drugs might have indirect effects on them as well. This could add to a wider effect on symptoms like mood swings and recklessness.

While the study on antiepileptic drugs for BPD is continuing, there are hopeful findings:

Meta-analyses (studies that examine the results of multiple clinical trials) show that specific antiepileptic drugs like lamotrigine (Lamictal), topiramate (Topamax), and divalproate (Depakote) can greatly lower emotional instability and recklessness in people with BPD. Some studies also suggest possible benefits in controlling other BPD symptoms like angry outbursts and self-harm behaviors.

Individual Studies: Research on lamotrigine is particularly hopeful, with some studies showing it might be even more effective than standard antidepressants in controlling borderline-related depression episodes. Additionally, topiramate might offer special benefits in lowering cravings for substances like booze and drugs, which can be a significant worry for some people with BPD.

One of the key benefits of antiepileptic drugs lies in their unique mode of action compared to antipsychotics, another medicine class used in BPD treatment.

Antipsychotics: These drugs mainly target dopamine D2 receptors and serotonin 5HT2A receptors in the brain. This can be successful in treating signs like mental upheaval, recklessness, and cognitive problems.

Antiepileptics: Their main action appears to involve controlling the activity of GABA and glutamate, the brain's major inhibiting and hyperactive chemicals, respectively. This process seems to be particularly helpful in controlling emotional instability and recklessness.

By utilizing different paths, antipsychotics and antiepileptic drugs can offer a combined approach to BPD treatment, possibly addressing a wider range of symptoms and raising the chance of getting therapeutic effects. For instance, some people might react better to the combined effects of both drug classes, while others might find sufficient symptom reduction with just one type of medication.

Tailoring Treatment: Exploring Individual Response and Side Effects

The three main antiepileptic drugs used in BPD treatment (lamotrigine, topiramate, and divalproate) have some unique features that can affect treatment decisions:

Lamictal (Lamotrigine): Lamictal also has a relatively good side-effect profile compared to other antiepileptic meds. However, it's crucial to be aware of a rare but dangerous skin rash that can appear, especially with a fast dose increase.

Topamax (Topiramate): Beyond its possible mood-stabilizing benefits, topiramate might also decrease cravings for food, booze, and drugs, which can be a major worry for some people with BPD. It's important to note that topiramate can also cause weight loss, which can be a benefit for some but a worry for others. Additionally, some people experience cognitive side effects like trouble with remembering and focusing at higher doses.

Depakote (Divalproate): While helpful for some, divalproate can cause significant weight gain, a possible side effect to consider when talking about treatment choices with your doctor. Divalproate can also interfere with other drugs, so it's important to reveal all medications you are taking to your doctor. There are also possible risks linked with birth problems if a woman becomes pregnant while taking divalproate, so women of childbearing age must talk about these risks with their doctor.

The Importance of Informed Consent: Off-Label Use and Shared Decision-Making

It's important to remember that these drugs are not currently FDA-approved for BPD treatment. They are considered "off-label use," meaning their success for BPD is backed by study but not formally cleared by the FDA. Therefore, it's important to have a full conversation with your therapist regarding the possible benefits and risks of any drug before beginning treatment. This talk should include:

• A review of your complaints and treatment goals.

• A full description of how antiepileptic drugs might work for BPD and the possible benefits you might experience.

• A description of the possible side effects of each drug and how they might impact you.

• A study of different treatment choices, including psychology and lifestyle changes.

The value of ongoing tracking is to measure the success of the medicine and handle any side effects.

By working closely with your therapist and making educated choices about your treatment plan, you can take an active part in your healing journey. While antiepileptic drugs can be a helpful tool, they are just one piece of the picture in BPD treatment. Here's a lesson of the value of a complete approach:

Psychotherapy: This remains the cornerstone of treatment, as it provides you with the skills to control your feelings, regulate behavior, and build healthy relationships. Different types of treatment, such as Dialectical Behavior treatment (DBT) and Mentalization-Based Therapy (MBT), are particularly helpful for BPD.

Lifestyle Changes: Developing healthy habits like regular exercise, proper sleep, and stress management methods can play a significant role in your general well-being. These living changes can help you manage your feelings, improve your happiness, and increase your resilience.

Support Groups: Connecting with others who understand the struggles of BPD can be a source of strength and support. Support groups can provide a safe place to share your stories, learn coping techniques, and feel less alone.

Anti-Anxiety Agents and Sedatives: A Cautious Approach in Borderline Personality Disorder Treatment

Benzodiazepines: A Weapon with Two Edges

Drugs of the benzodiazepine family, which includes clonazepam (Klonopin), lorazepam (Ativan), diazepam (Valium), and alprazolam (Xanax), are frequently used to treat anxiety and sleep problems. They function by amplifying the tranquil and relaxing effects of gamma-aminobutyric acid (GABA), a brain neurotransmitter.

While benzodiazepines can help some people with BPD sleep better and experience brief respite from anxiety, using them has serious side effects:

High Potential for Addiction: The potential for addiction to benzodiazepines is one of the most worrying features of these drugs. Benzodiazepines can increase the likelihood of impulsive behaviors in those with BPD, who are already predisposed to them. When a drug is used for an extended period, dependency can develop, making it difficult to stop using it without suffering withdrawal symptoms.

Increased Impulsivity: According to research, some BPD patients can paradoxically become more impulsive while using benzodiazepines. This can exacerbate the main symptoms of BPD and cause dangerous or self-destructive behavior.

Tolerance and Dependency: The body can become tolerant to benzodiazepines over time, requiring larger and higher dosages to have the same effects. This raises the possibility of dependency and withdrawal symptoms while quitting even higher.

Other Benzodiazepine Medications for Anxiety and Sleep

Alternative drugs and techniques can be investigated in light of benzodiazepine safety concerns to treat anxiety and sleep disruptions in individuals with BPD:

(Buspar) Buspirone: This non-benzodiazepine medicine reduces anxiety symptoms differently. Compared to benzodiazepines, it has a lesser risk of addiction, although it can take a few weeks to get the full benefits.

• *Antidepressants:* Since anxiety and depression often co-occur with BPD, certain antidepressants, such as selective serotonin reuptake inhibitors (SSRIs), can help manage both conditions.

• *CBT, or cognitive behavioral therapy:* Through this kind of treatment, patients can learn to recognize and confront the unfavorable thinking patterns that fuel their worry. Long-term management of anxiety symptoms can be greatly aided by CBT.

• *Sleep Hygiene Practices:* You can greatly enhance the quality of your sleep by adopting healthy sleep hygiene practices, which include sticking to a regular sleep schedule, setting up a soothing bedtime ritual, and using relaxation methods before bed.

Concerns About Non-Benzodiazepine Sedatives: Zolpidem (Ambien)

Another drug that is sometimes used for sleep problems is zolpidem (Ambien). It's not a benzodiazepine, but its hazards are comparable. Some BPD sufferers can have paradoxical effects on zolpidem, such as:

• *Aggression:* Zolpidem can, in some BPD patients, elicit violent behavior as opposed to encouraging calm.

• *Extroversion:* The drug can surprisingly make you more chatty and have trouble falling asleep.

• *Agitation:* Rather than encouraging sleep, zolpidem might sometimes exacerbate agitation and restlessness.

• *Hallucinations:* An uncommon but very upsetting adverse effect of zolpidem is the induction of hallucinations.

• *Depersonalization:* Some zolpidem users report feeling detached from their environment or themselves.

A Tailored Strategy: Collaborating with your medical group

It's important to address anxiety and sleep issues with your healthcare team if you experience them as a result of your BPD. Together, you can investigate a customized treatment plan that takes into account the advantages and disadvantages of several drug possibilities while attending to your requirements. Here's what to anticipate:

Entire Assessment: To fully understand your BPD symptoms, medical history, and any other drugs you can be taking, your doctor will do a complete assessment.

Cooperative Decision-Making: Your doctor will walk you through the possible advantages and disadvantages of several treatment choices, both medication- and non-medication-based, so you can actively take part in making decisions about your care.

Put Long-Term Solutions First: The objective is to reduce dependency on potentially addictive drugs by finding long-term alternatives for the efficient management of anxiety and sleep problems. If required, this can include a mix of lifestyle modifications, psychotherapy, and carefully chosen drugs.

For the long-term treatment of anxiety and sleep issues in individuals with BPD, a more all-encompassing strategy is essential, even if anti-anxiety medications and sedatives can provide some respite. Here's a rundown of the main conclusions:

• ***Pay Attention to Underlying Issues:*** Emotional dysregulation is often the root cause of BPD. Reducing anxiety and improving sleep quality can be accomplished by addressing these fundamental concerns via psychotherapy such as Mentalization-Based Therapy (MBT) or Dialectical Behavior Therapy (DBT).

• ***Lifestyle Changes:*** Adopting healthful routines can greatly reduce anxiety and enhance sleep. Improved emotional control and better sleep can be facilitated by regular exercise, mindfulness meditation, and the establishment of a regular sleep routine.

• ***Mind-Body Methods:*** Methods such as deep breathing techniques, yoga, and progressive muscle relaxation can help induce calm and lessen the symptoms of anxiety.

• ***Supportive Network:*** Anxiety and sleep problems can be caused by stress, which can be managed and emotional validation can be obtained from friends, family, or a therapist.

Antidepressants: A Targeted Approach for Mood Regulation and Sleep Improvement in BPD

Antidepressants address particular symptoms of Borderline Personality Disorder (BPD) and enhance general well-being, making them an effective tool in controlling the condition. Here's a deeper look at their potential advantages for people with BPD:

1. Mood Swing Regulation: BPD is characterized by strong, fast-changing emotions. Antidepressants of certain kinds can lessen the frequency and intensity of emotional swings while also aiding in mood stabilization. Here are a few instances:

SSRIs, or selective serotonin reuptake inhibitors: These drugs, which include escitalopram (Lexapro), sertraline (Zoloft), and fluoxetine (Prozac), function by making more serotonin, a neurotransmitter that helps control mood, available in the brain. SSRIs can help people with BPD have more stable moods and exhibit less emotional reactivity by raising serotonin levels.

Serotonin-Norepinephrine Reuptake Inhibitors (SNRIs): These drugs work on serotonin as well as norepinephrine, another neurotransmitter that is important in mood regulation. Examples of SNRIs are venlafaxine (Effexor) and duloxetine (Cymbalta). SNRIs can be especially beneficial for those who are experiencing co-occurring anxiety and depression, which are frequent BPD symptoms.

2. Diminished Depression: BPD and depression often coexist, making it more difficult to manage emotions and go about everyday tasks. Antidepressants are an effective treatment for BPD's depressed symptoms.

Minimizing Negativism and Depression: Antidepressants work by controlling neurotransmitter levels, which can elevate mood, lessen despondency, and boost motivation.

Increasing Energy Levels: Fatigue and low energy are common side effects of depression. Antidepressants can increase energy levels, which enables BPD sufferers to participate more fully in everyday activities and treatment.

Encouraging Better Sleep: Sleep habits can be disturbed by depression. Certain antidepressants enhance the quality of sleep, which benefits mood and general wellbeing.

3. Possible Enhancement of Sleep Quality: Although not all antidepressants aid in sleep directly, several do so indirectly by resolving underlying problems:

Reducing Anxiety: Sleep disruptions are significantly influenced by anxiety. SNRIs in particular are antidepressants that can help control anxiety symptoms, which promotes better sleep and a more tranquil mood.

Relieving Depression Symptoms: As was previously indicated, depression can cause irregular sleep patterns. Antidepressants have an indirect positive impact on improved sleep hygiene since they elevate mood and lessen depressed symptoms.

Choosing the Correct Drug: Antidepressants function differently and have a range of negative effects. To optimize benefits and reduce side effects, it is essential to collaborate with your doctor in selecting the appropriate drug and dose.

Combination Therapy: For a more thorough course of therapy, it can sometimes be required to combine an antidepressant with another drug, such as an antipsychotic to address impulsivity.

The Key Is Therapy: The best results from antidepressants are obtained when combined with psychotherapy, such as dialectical behavior therapy (DBT). Individuals with Borderline Personality Disorder (BPD) can learn effective coping strategies, regulate their behavior, and control their emotions via therapy.

Working together with your healthcare team and being aware of the possible advantages of antidepressants can help you choose whether or not this class of medications is a good match for controlling your symptoms of borderline personality disorder and enhancing your general health. Although borderline personality disorder can be difficult to treat, there are ways to help. Together with your healthcare team, you can control anxiety and sleep disruptions, enhance your general health, and lead a satisfying life by taking a holistic approach. Rehab is a journey, so keep in mind that there will be ups and downs. But you can create a better future for yourself if you work hard, are kind to yourself, and have the correct support network.

Nutritional Support: The Role of Diet and Supplements in Neurotransmitter Balance for Borderline Personality Disorder (BPD)

Although psychotherapy is still the mainstay of treatment for borderline personality disorder (BPD), an increasing amount of evidence indicates that nutritional supplementation might help address the disorder's basic symptoms. People with Borderline Personality Disorder (BPD) can benefit from targeted supplements and a balanced, nutrient-rich diet to help with emotional control, mood stability, and general well-being. The intriguing relationship between food, neurotransmitters, and BPD is examined in this section.

The Brain-Gut Relationship:

The large population of microbes that live in our digestive systems, known as the gut microbiome, is essential to both mental and digestive health. Current studies demonstrate a two-way communication channel between the brain and the stomach, known as the "gut-brain axis." Stress and emotional states can affect the makeup of the gut microbiota, and the gut microbiome can affect brain function by producing neurotransmitters. Chemical messengers called neurotransmitters let neurons communicate with one another in the brain. It's believed that certain neurotransmitter imbalances have a role in the BPD symptoms. The following lists the main neurotransmitters and how they relate to BPD:

• *Serotonin:* This neurotransmitter is sometimes referred to as the "feel-good" molecule because of its important functions in hunger, sleep, and mood control. Low serotonin levels are linked to frequent BPD symptoms such as impulsivity, anxiety, and sadness.

• *Dopamine:* Dopamine plays a role in pleasure processing, reward seeking, and motivation. Dopamine dysregulation can be a factor in impulsive actions and trouble feeling happy in people with BPD.

• *GABA:* This neurotransmitter promotes relaxation and serenity by acting as an inhibitory neurotransmitter. Increased emotional reactivity and difficulty settling down in BPD can be related to insufficient GABA activation.

• *Glutamate:* The brain's main excitatory neurotransmitter, glutamate is involved in mood regulation, memory, and learning. BPD is characterized by emotional instability and impulsivity, which can be related to excessive glutamate activation.

Nutritional Techniques to Promote Neurotransmitter Equilibrium

Through dietary modifications, it can be possible to promote the synthesis and functionality of several important neurotransmitters:

• *Reuptake Inhibitors:* Foods high in tryptophan, which is a building block of serotonin, can be advantageous. Fish, poultry, eggs, beans, nuts, and seeds are a few examples. Consuming complex carbs, such as whole grains, can also support stable blood sugar levels, which in turn affects serotonin synthesis indirectly.

• *Dopamine Support:* The body uses the amino acid tyrosine to produce dopamine. Tyrosine for dopamine synthesis can be obtained from meals including chicken, fish, dairy products, beans, avocados, and bananas.

• ***Encouraging GABA Function:*** Precursors for the synthesis of GABA are present in several meals. These include vitamin B6-rich foods and vegetables including bananas, sweet potatoes, and leafy greens. Furthermore, eating foods that have undergone fermentation, such as kefir and yogurt, might maintain a healthy gut flora, which can, in turn, improve GABA function.

• ***Regulation of Glutamate:*** Glutamate is necessary, but too much of it can be harmful. Reducing added sugars, processed meals, and refined carbs can help control glutamate levels. Furthermore, there can be a balancing impact from emphasizing the omega-3 fatty acids, which are present in walnuts, flaxseeds, and fatty fish.

Taking into Account Targeted Supplementation: Speaking with a Medical Expert

A balanced diet is important, however, some people with BPD can benefit from particular neurotransmitter shortages addressed by tailored supplements. Still, it's crucial to speak with a licensed healthcare provider before beginning any supplementation. Here's something to think about:

Customized Evaluation: Through blood tests or other diagnostic procedures, a doctor can determine your requirements and probable shortcomings. They can offer suitable vitamins and doses based on this evaluation.

Supplement Quality: There is a wide range in the purity and quality of supplements. You can get advice from your doctor on reliable brands and premium formulas.

Possible Interactions: Supplements and any drugs you can be taking can interact. To prevent any negative interactions, you must tell your doctor about all of your drugs and supplements.

Remember: Psychotherapy and a well-balanced diet cannot be replaced by supplements. When dietary modifications alone can not be enough, they are meant to provide further assistance.

Here are some additional points to consider when incorporating nutritional support into your BPD management plan:

Creating Healthful Habits: Put your attention on creating gratifying and long-lasting dietary adjustments. Steer clear of restrictive fad diets and aim for a range of meals high in nutrients.

Develop a positive connection with food by engaging in mindful eating practices. Take note of your body's signals of hunger and fullness, and enjoy the act of eating.

The Value of Working as a Team and Being Consistent

The Value of Uniformity Sustaining regular dietary modifications is essential for long-term advantages. Don't let the odd mistake demotivate you. Consider their educational opportunities and make a fresh commitment to your nutritious diet.

Working as a Team: You can choose to work with a nutritionist or registered dietitian who specializes in mental health. They can provide you with individualized meal planning advice, point out any nutritional deficits, and work with you to create a long-term strategy for nutritional support for your BPD.

The optimal combination for nutritional assistance is evidence-based treatments such as Dialectical Behavior Therapy (DBT). DBT gives people with BPD the tools they need to effectively communicate with others, manage their emotions, tolerate discomfort, and practice mindfulness. DBT can assist you in recognizing the emotional triggers that can result in unhealthy eating patterns. For instance, when you're feeling stressed out, you could go for comfort food. It is possible to create more healthful coping strategies for emotional discomfort by fusing DBT techniques with dietary understanding. Mindfulness is emphasized in DBT, and it can be used in mindful eating. You can prevent emotional eating and make more thoughtful food choices by being aware of your body's signals of hunger and fullness. A robust support network can be advantageous for both DBT and a nutritious diet. Counselors can assist you in creating positive connections, and a trained dietitian can provide guidance when it comes to handling social situations involving food.

This chapter has covered a lot of territory in terms of discussing various approaches to treating borderline personality disorder (BPD). However, cultivating wholesome connections is an additional crucial component of the jigsaw. It might sometimes be difficult to connect with others the way you would want to if you have BPD symptoms.

Even while this chapter's ideas provide helpful skills for controlling BPD symptoms, genuine empowerment comes from going beyond symptom management to include self-discovery and finding your inner strength. The purpose of the next chapter, "Strength in Vulnerability: Building on Your Assets," is to help you build a more objective viewpoint, recognize your strengths, and cultivate self-compassion instead of just managing obstacles. Even with BPD, you can establish a basis for wholesome relationships and a happy life by accepting your weaknesses and enhancing your special traits.

CHAPTER 8

Strength in Vulnerability: Building on Your Assets

For a brief instant, see vulnerability as a source of power rather than a weakness. It's the guts to be real, own your shortcomings, and establish genuine connections with others. Building solid, sustaining connections is a crucial component of surviving borderline personality disorder (BPD), and this vulnerability serves as the basis for these partnerships.

This chapter adopts a different strategy than the previous ones, which concentrates on giving you the skills you need to manage the symptoms of BPD. We'll go on a self-discovery adventure here, learning how to strengthen your inner self and lay the groundwork for happy relationships.

Find Your Strengths and Let Your Light Shine: Realizing Your Worth

Sometimes your innate abilities and capabilities might be overshadowed by BPD. You could catch yourself making negative comparisons to other people or obsessing about perceived shortcomings. This can damage your capacity to connect with others truly and result in poor self-esteem. The fact is that you possess a special set of abilities and qualities that are just waiting to be unlocked! We'll look at activities to assist you in determining your:

Strengths: What skills come easily to you? Are you imaginative, kind, methodical, witty, or an excellent listener? Acknowledging your strengths can help you become more self-assured and enable you to bring your special talents to your relationships. Maybe you're good at solving puzzles, or maybe you have a way of making others laugh in awkward situations or feel noticed and comfortable. Finding these abilities enables you to share them with others, resulting in stronger bonds and deeper connections.

Skills: Is there anything you're secretly good at writing, cooking, performing music, or making others laugh? Finding and developing your abilities can make you happier and more fulfilled, which will make you a more fascinating and engaging person to interact with. Perhaps you have a gift for writing moving poetry, a love of creating delectable foods, or a lovely singing voice that you haven't shared. Possessing these skills can make you happy personally and help you make connections with like-minded others.

Special Qualities: What qualities do you provide to relationships? Are you a trustworthy confidante, an encouraging spouse, a devoted friend, or a funny person? Comprehending your distinct contributions might aid in acknowledging your significance in the lives of others. Maybe you are the one who always stands by your friends in difficult times, creates a secure environment where your spouse can be vulnerable, or infuses joy and lightness into any event. Acknowledging these contributions enables you to strengthen your relationships and appreciate your position in your loved ones' lives.

Realizing your worth on the inside will give you the courage to interact with others more genuinely. You'll be able to openly share your skills and qualities with others, creating stronger bonds and deeper connections.

Accept Yourself: Be Your Own Best Friend

Treating oneself with love and empathy, as you would a good friend going through a difficult moment, is the essence of self-compassion. Let's say your buddy is experiencing anxiety or overload. What kind of words of support and encouragement would you give? Now show yourself the same consideration.

Here are a few tactics that you can employ:

Dispute Your Negative Self Talk: Recognize when negative ideas are taking over and take action to stop them. Are these ideas constructive or realistic? You could be thinking to yourself, "I'm a burden to everyone around me." Dispute this idea by highlighting your good traits and the assistance you provide to others.

Put mindfulness into practice: You can become more objectively aware of your thoughts and emotions by practicing mindfulness. You can control how you react instead of letting your emotions control you if you can see them objectively. You can learn to silence your inner critic and make room for self-compassion by practicing mindfulness exercises like meditation.

Concentrate on Your Development: Don't let failures depress you. No matter how little your progress is, acknowledge it. Perhaps you confronted a bad notion for the first time or discovered a strength you hadn't previously considered. Acknowledging these advancements encourages you to keep going on your self-discovery path and fosters self-compassion.

It is simpler to create wholesome connections with other people when you learn to treat yourself with kindness. You'll attract folks who value your sincerity by exuding a more upbeat and self-assured vibe. Self-compassion makes it possible for you to establish more vulnerable and trusting connections with others.

Establishing Sound Perceptions and Acquiring the Ability to Describe People Objectively

How we interact with people and ourselves is greatly influenced by our impressions of them. Sometimes, BPD can result in warped perspectives, which makes it challenging to establish wholesome connections. You could, for instance, idealize someone one minute and hate them the next, resulting in dynamics that are unstable and unpredictable. You will get strategies in this chapter to help you cultivate a more objective viewpoint and better relationships. Let's look at the following:

Recognizing Cognitive Errors Negative thought patterns known as cognitive distortions have the power to warp your sense of reality. We'll learn to recognize typical cognitive distortions linked to borderline personality disorder (BPD), such as emotional reasoning ("I feel angry, therefore they must hate me") and all-or-nothing thinking ("If I'm not perfect, I'm a complete failure"). You can confront these illusions and cultivate more impartial perspectives of both yourself and other people by being aware of them.

Distinguishing Feelings from Reality: Sometimes having BPD makes it hard to distinguish between facts and feelings. A neutral remark might be interpreted as a personal assault, which could cause miscommunication and conflict. We'll look at methods for separating your subjective world from your emotional responses. By doing this, you'll be able to react to circumstances more logically and strengthen your bonds with others.

Taking Into Account Various Views: It's easy to lose sight of the wider picture when you get mired in your viewpoint. We'll help you become better at taking other people's perspectives into account. You can encourage more courteous and cooperative relationships by engaging in empathy practices and trying to comprehend other people's perspectives.

Gaining an objective viewpoint can help you negotiate tricky social situations, gain people's trust, and create enduring, healthy connections. Recall that being vulnerable doesn't mean being weak; rather, it means accepting who you really are and developing stronger connections with others. You will be able to develop self-compassion, build on your strengths, and nurture healthy perspectives using the skills and tactics covered in this chapter. These are all necessary components for successful relationships and a meaningful life with BPD.

Top Qualities of BPD Patients

Deep Empathy and Compassion: Individuals with BPD can be very adept at really comprehending and empathizing with the emotions of others. They can be extraordinarily devoted and helpful friends, spouses, or family members because of their keen sense of empathy.

Passion and Creativity: BPD patients can express their feelings via writing, music, painting, or other creative mediums. Not only can they inspire and beautify themselves, but also everyone around them, when they use their creativity. Their enthusiasm can be infectious, as can their zeal for life and impassioned activities.

Strength and Resilience: Although having BPD can make everyday life difficult, it can also promote remarkable resilience. In order to deal with challenging emotions and circumstances, people with BPD often develop robust coping strategies and a strong sense of inner power.

Intensity and Authenticity: Individuals with borderline personality disorder (BPD) often have strong emotional experiences. Although this can be challenging at times, it can also result in a sincere and passionate style of relating to others. They can be quite devoted and provide a distinctive viewpoint to relationships, which makes them fascinating and captivating companions.

Sensitivity and Intuition: BPD can cause heightened awareness of other people's feelings and needs. As a result, they can become observant companions or lovers who can read nonverbal clues and provide a depth of comprehension that others would overlook.

High Emotional Intelligence: Adding to what was said before, individuals with BPD often have high emotional intelligence. They can handle social circumstances with a deeper knowledge since they are very aware of both their own and other people's emotions.

Openness to Experience: BPD can sometimes result in an increased receptivity to new experiences. It's possible that those who have BPD are more open to trying new things, considering many viewpoints, and accepting the whole gamut of human emotions. They can be fascinating lovers and pals because of their openness.

Determinate and Persistent: When they put their minds to something they believe in, people with BPD can be very determined and persistent. This tenacity can be a great help in accomplishing objectives and overcoming obstacles.

Independent and Self-Reliant: Borderline Personality Disorder (BPD) can promote independence and self-reliance in addition to a fear of abandonment. Individuals with BPD can discover inner strength and acquire coping mechanisms for challenging emotions.

Strong Sense of Identity: Although some people with BPD struggle with their sense of self, others can grow to have a strong sense of who they are as a result of how intensely they feel and see the world. This distinct viewpoint has the potential to inspire creativity and power.

FINAL NOTE

When you close this book, it seems like the end. You've taken on an important responsibility by learning how to control your BPD and create enduring relationships. That is indeed something to be very pleased about!

Do you recall your first feelings when you began reading? Perhaps a bit disoriented, perplexed, or even irritated. You were courageous enough to ask for assistance since those emotions were genuine. See how far you've come now! You've gained some incredible abilities that will enable you to succeed in life. Finding your strengths—the things that make you unique—is among the greatest things you've learned. It's your creativity that adds a special spark to your life, your loyalty that makes you a trustworthy friend, or your sense of humor that makes others laugh. Acknowledging these assets increases your self-assurance and enables you to impart them to others, strengthening and enriching your connections. You didn't stop there, however. You also discovered the value of treating yourself with kindness, especially on difficult days. It's similar to having a supportive and understanding internal cheerleader. You can weather emotional storms more gracefully and recover from failures more quickly when you practice self-compassion. No matter how little your victory can be, you should enjoy it because you deserve it!

Above all, you developed positive interpersonal relationships. You came to understand the value of honest self-expression and attentive listening in clear communication. Establishing a bridge of understanding, promotes solid, encouraging connections based on respect for one another. Unexpected events do occur in life. There will be moments when communication becomes difficult or emotions get jumbled. That's OK! The good news is that you are no longer alone. You now have the tools in this book to deal with these circumstances.

Are you feeling overpowered? You gained knowledge about how to locate your center and relax with mindfulness. Are you stuck thinking bad thoughts? You can confront them with constructive self-talk and adopt a more optimistic outlook. Desire more solid relationships? You are aware of the ability to communicate honestly and openly to express yourself freely and establish trust. Recall that while BPD affects you, it does not rule your life. You have what it takes to create a happy, loving, and meaningful future for yourself. You are strong, competent, and prepared. You are the writer of your own life, and every action you do will help you create a better future for yourself.

Keep going, acknowledge and enjoy your victories, no matter how tiny, and accept the incredible person you are growing into. This is something you can handle! These teachings provide the groundwork for an exciting future. Now that you have the necessary knowledge and abilities, you can design a life that really expresses who you are. So go off, shine your light, and enjoy the amazing ride that lies ahead of you!

Did This Book Help You? Share Your Experience!

The adventure of this book doesn't finish here! If the techniques and resources you acquired from these pages have helped you manage your BPD and create enduring relationships, you can want to consider sharing your story with others.

By giving a sincere review on Amazon, you can motivate others going through similar struggles and engage with a larger community.

The following is how to write a review:

- Go to the Amazon website for the book.
- Search for the area labeled "Write a customer review".
- Tell us about the book's usefulness, understanding, and general influence on your experience with BPD.

For someone looking for direction and assistance, your frank assessment would really make a difference.

I appreciate you taking the time to read!

ABOUT AUTHOR

Dr. Riley Thompson Brooks is a licensed psychotherapist with extensive experience guiding individuals through the complexities of mental health challenges. Her dedication to her patients and their well-being shines through in her compassionate approach and evidence-based practices.

Dr. Brooks has worked with a wide range of mental disorders, including Borderline Personality Disorder (BPD). Through her work, she has helped countless individuals navigate their emotions, build healthy relationships, and create fulfilling lives.

Driven by a desire to reach a wider audience and empower more people on their journeys, Dr. Brooks translates her clinical expertise into accessible and informative books. Her writing style is clear, compassionate, and practical, offering readers clear tools and strategies for managing their mental health.

Beyond her professional life, Dr. Brooks finds immense joy in her personal life. She is a happily married woman and a proud mother of three emotionally healthy children. This personal experience allows her to understand the unique challenges and triumphs faced by individuals and families navigating mental health challenges.

Dr. Brooks' commitment to her patients, her passion for mental health awareness, and her dedication to empowering others through writing make her a valuable resource for anyone seeking guidance and support.